The Art of HEARTHSTONE

Volume V:
Year of the Dragon

TITAN BOOKS

BLIZZARD ENTERTAINMENT

BLIZZARD ENTERTAINMENT
Written By: Robert Brooks
Editor: Jake Gerli
Game Team Direction: Jeremy Cranford, Linus Flink, Bree Lawlor
Lore Consultation: Madi Buckingham, Sean Copeland, Justin Parker
Production: Brianne Messina, Derek Rosenberg, Anna Wan
Director, Consumer Products: Byron Parnell
Director, Creative Development: David Seeholzer

DESIGN BY CAMERON + COMPANY
Publisher: Chris Gruener
Creative Director: Iain R. Morris
Art Director: Suzi Hutsell
Designer: Rob Dolgaard & Amy Wheless

© 2021 Blizzard Entertainment, Inc. Blizzard and the Blizzard Entertainment logo are trademarks or registered trademarks of Blizzard Entertainment, Inc. in the U.S. or other countries.

Published by Titan Books, London, in 2021.

Published by arrangement with Blizzard Entertainment, Inc., Irvine, California.

TITAN BOOKS

A division of Titan Publishing Group Ltd

144 Southwark Street. London SE1 0UP

www.titanbooks.com

Find us on Facebook: www.facebook.com/titanbooks

Follow us on Twitter: @TitanBooks

A CIP catalogue record for this title is available from the British Library.

ISBN: 978-1789098457

Manufactured in China

PAGE 1 Lazul Madame/Tarot Card - Peter Stapleton
PREVIOUS PAGE Dragons - MAR Studio
RIGHT Ludo Lullabi & Sam Nielson
FOLLOWING PAGE MAR Studio

CONTENTS

FOREWORD ◆ 8

INTRODUCTION ◆ 10

1. **YEAR OF THE DRAGON** ◆ 13
2. **RISE OF SHADOWS** ◆ 18
3. **SAVIORS OF ULDUM** ◆ 86
4. **DESCENT OF DRAGONS** ◆ 152
5. **NEW FRONTIERS** ◆ 232

CONCLUSION ◆ 246

FOREWORD
A Yearlong Narrative

I still remember how excited I was when I heard about the plan for the yearlong narrative eventually named the Year of the Dragon. In this story, the villains from our past expansions would form a supervillain group called the League of E.V.I.L. and compete against the League of Explorers.

This was a new direction for the *Hearthstone* team, and we always seem to shine when we try something new. I had only one request: I wanted to bring back the troll fortune-teller from the *Whispers of the Old Gods* cinematic and have her join the E.V.I.L team. Everyone supported the idea. She would be named Madame Lazul and would become the fifth villain, along with Rafaam, Togwaggle, Hagatha, and Dr. Boom.

The next decision was to determine the plans for the E.V.I.L. villains. According to former lead narrative designer Dave Kosak, the villains needed to do something big, and it was suggested they steal the entire city of Dalaran. This became act 1 of the story that would play out in the *Rise of Shadows* expansion where players would first see Dr. Boom in his new flying mech suit.

The story continued in the *Saviors of Uldum* expansion, which featured the League of Explorers in their new desert gear, designed by principal artist Jerry Mascho specifically for the expansion (see page 102). This set also led to the creation of one of the most memorable moments in Hearthstone cinematics—when Reno Jackson does the splits while riding a camel. Internally, this scene is referred to as the "flexplosion" scene. I also loved all the classic dungeon traps shown on cards like **Pressure Plate** and **Flame Wand**.

The Year of the Dragon was not without its creative challenges. One obstacle the team had to overcome was to determine Reno Jackson's class. There was a strong desire for him to be a mage, but he is too impatient to study and learn spells. We had to come up with a solution that fit the story line. It was suggested that maybe Reno could discover an ancient artifact that allows him to cast spells without actually learning any magic. Something like a wand but much more epic: the Gatling Wand. Once Reno discovered the Gatling Wand, he could cast spells and become a mage. Of course, all the Kirin Tor turned up their noses at him viewing him more as a thief than a mage. It was done.

The final expansion introduced the largest dragon ever known in the *World of Warcraft* universe, Galakrond. But we didn't want just any Galakrond; we designed our Galakrond to be able to evolve, get more powerful over time, and become your hero if you play a priest, rogue, shaman, warlock, or warrior deck. You can see some of Christopher Hayes's early concepts for the Galakrond evolution on page 174.

All the excitement culminated in an epic air battle in the *Descent of Dragons* expansion. This set has more dragon cards than any other *Hearthstone* expansion.

So sit back and enjoy many of the very best paintings created for this vast story line. I have a feeling we have not seen the last of the League of E.V.I.L. . . .

—Jeremy Cranford

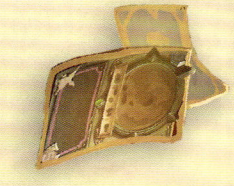

INTRODUCTION
WELCOME BACK, FRIEND!

You're back! And your timing couldn't be more perfect. I came up with a new riddle tonight, and the folks in the tavern have been arguing about the answer.

Let's see what you think: "I come in different hues: black, green, red, yellow, and blue. I walk on four legs, or none, or two. What am I?"

That's right! A dragon! They can walk on all fours, they can fly, and they can change into a mortal that walks on two legs! It's the bit about the colors that gives the answer away, innit?

But try telling that to those five sinister folks sitting in the corner. You see them, right? The guy with the bandages, the goblin with the hood, the orc who smells like a swamp, the kobold with no gold, and the troll fortune-teller holding her pet snake? She can literally see the future, so she knows the answer, but they're still debating with her about it! I wonder if they're capable of agreeing on anything, honestly.

They really are a strange crew. Don't tell anyone, but I think they might be criminals. I heard them planning some sort of heist. The one with the cloth wrappings around his face keeps breaking into song when he talks about it.

They might actually be looking for recruits. Normally, I wouldn't recommend grouping up with such unsavory sorts, but I have a funny feeling about them. Maybe they're worth joining, if only for a little while.

I heard they might start their adventure with a trip to Dalaran.

Then they might take a detour toward Uldum. Wonder what's out there in that desert . . .

But their ultimate goal seems to be far in the north, up in the icy winds of Northrend. It's been too long since I've had some fun in the snow!

Want to tag along with them? Who knows what sorts of adventures we can find . . .

—Harth Stonebrew, the Innkeeper

OPPOSITE
Ludo Lullabi & Sam Nielson

1

YEAR OF THE DRAGON

You are just in time to witness the culmination of my genius!

—Rafaam

LOFTY AMBITIONS

For five years, the *Hearthstone* team had been building their own expression of the *Warcraft* universe. "Fifteen degrees off of *Warcraft*" had been a guiding pillar since the early days of development, allowing the team to draw from its rich visual foundations without being closely bound by its lore, its characters, or its chronology.

It also allowed them to indulge in the sillier side of *Warcraft* whenever it felt appropriate.

When the team wanted to reimagine the rivalry between Nefarian and Ragnaros as a petty grudge match between disgruntled roommates, they did so in the game's second adventure, *Blackrock Mountain*. The haunted tower within Deadwind Pass was depicted as the ultimate party club in *One Night in Karazhan*. The gloomy city of Gilneas came under assault not from a Forsaken invasion but from the corrupted monsters lurking within the haunted forest of *The Witchwood*.

Along the way, the team created its own gallery of heroes, its own stable of villains, and its own unique voice.

Some popular characters, like Brann Bronzebeard, originated in *World of Warcraft* but became equally memorable to *Hearthstone* players because of their impact on the meta. Some villains, like Rafaam, were created by the *Hearthstone* team and quickly became fan favorites.

"We live in the *Warcraft* world, but we tell our own stories within it," said senior designer Chadd Nervig. "We ended up creating so many one-off characters just for single expansions, and after a while we asked, 'Can we use them to make a story that is truly our own?'"

PREVIOUS PAGE
MAR Studio

RIGHT & OPPOSITE
Ludo Lullabi

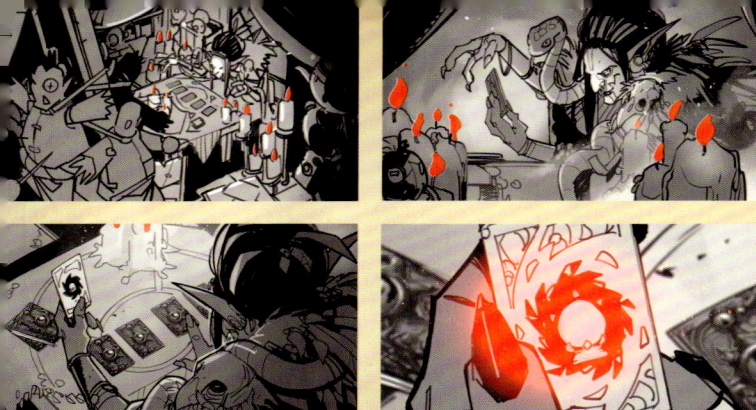

Eagle-eyed *Hearthstone* players have noticed that several unique characters made unexpected returns to the game in the years leading up to 2019. For instance, Elise Starseeker returned in the Year of the Mammoth (2017), while Dr. Boom got a starring role in his own expansion in the Year of the Raven (2018).

This was not an accident.

"It was definitely a deliberate Easter egg hunt for our players," said senior narrative designer Valerie Chu. "We had fun watching people on the internet put the pieces together, and some of them had a pretty good idea of what we were building."

When the team made card sets for 2018, they were laying the foundation for a big new initiative in 2019: an entire year of content driven by characters they had created themselves.

Perhaps more importantly, they wanted the year to be part of one continuous narrative: all three card sets would tell a complete story, culminating in a gigantic year-end climax.

It was ambitious. It was unprecedented for *Hearthstone*. And it would require the biggest year of content the game had ever had.

Three full expansion sets. Three adventure modes with very different mechanics. Limited-time events between expansions. And if that wasn't enough, *Hearthstone*'s designers would design, prototype, and ship an entirely new game mode called Battlegrounds amid it all.

This was the Year of the Dragon, one of the most exciting projects in *Hearthstone*'s history.

ABOVE & OPPOSITE
Ludo Lullabi

LEFT
Jomaro Kindred

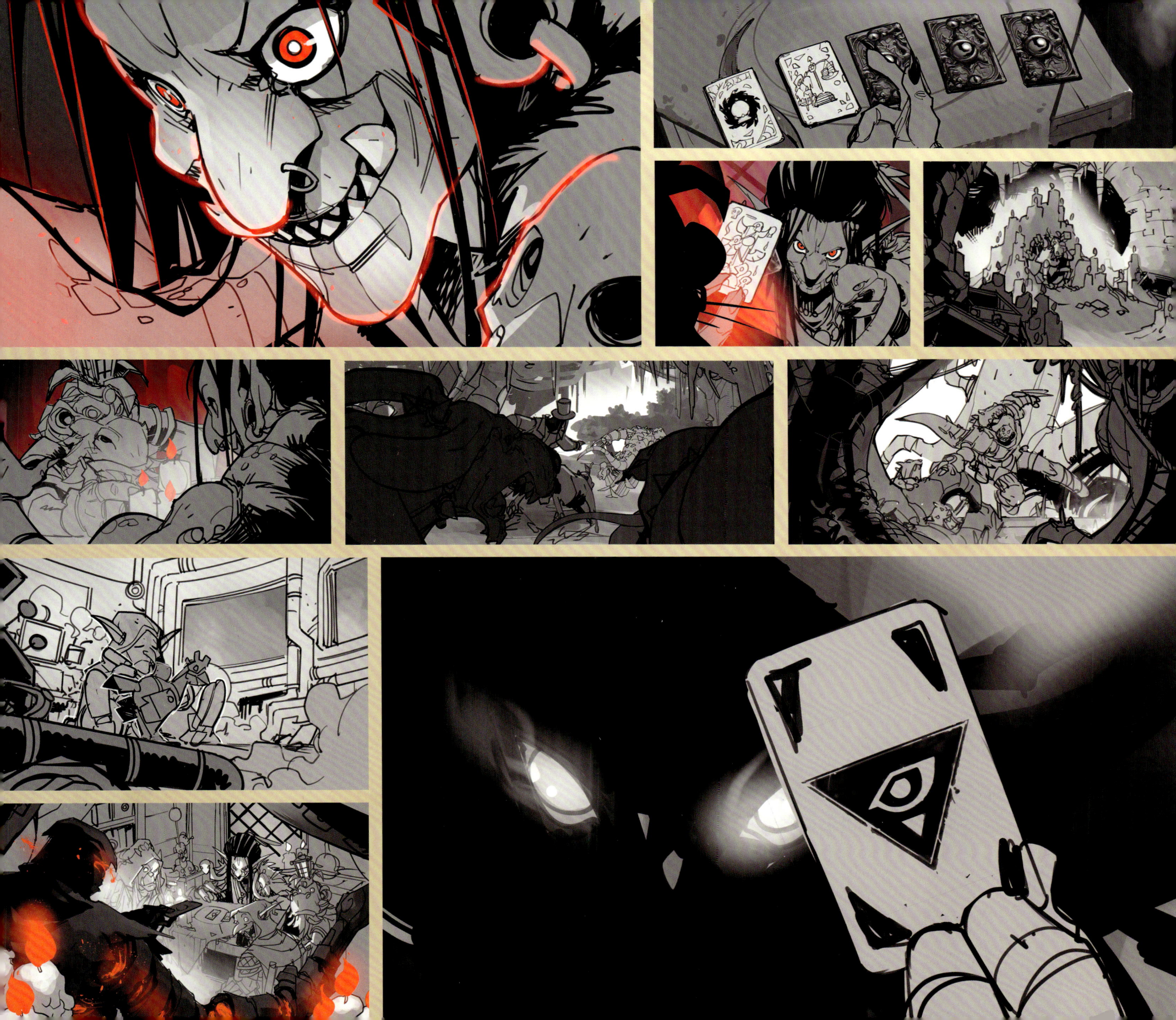

2

RISE OF SHADOWS

Now here's the plot to capture your greed and intrigue. We'll take Dalaran for all that it's got . . .

—Rafaam

RISE OF SHADOWS SHOW LEADERSHIP

DIRECTOR Jeramiah Johnson
DIRECTOR Brian Horn
PRODUCER Rachel Richmond
DFX SUPERVISOR David Satchwell
ART LEAD Sam Nielson

A MOTLEY CREW

Three and a half years before the Year of the Dragon, Brann Bronzebeard and his colleagues from the League of Explorers battled the villain Rafaam, the Supreme Archaeologist, who sought to claim a powerful artifact and rule the world. The good guys triumphed, the world was saved, and Rafaam limped away to lick his wounds and reflect on his mistakes.

It didn't take long for him to understand his biggest blunder: trying to conquer the world alone. He had been outnumbered. What if Rafaam had a loyal team at his side? What if he brought together the most powerful, smart, and capable people on Azeroth to fulfill his lifelong dreams?

We'll never know. The most powerful people on Azeroth were grinding for loot in groups of ten to twenty-five people.

But Rafaam didn't give up. Four other *Hearthstone* villains had free time on their schedules and were willing to join his League of E.V.I.L., which would change the balance of power forever.

PREVIOUS PAGE
Maximilian Degen

RIGHT
Max Grecke

Leading up to the Year of the Dragon, the Blizzard cinematics team released a series of teasers showing Rafaam's new crew receiving their invitations. They were: **Madame Lazul**, the mysterious troll fortune-teller who narrated the *Whispers of the Old Gods* cinematic in 2016; **King Togwaggle**, the ruler of a plundered kobold empire; **Hagatha**, the shaman who cursed the forests near Gilneas; and **Dr. Boom**, the eccentric pyromaniac who may or may not have blown up his own lab through his reckless experiments.

Rafaam taught them the power of friendship and musical numbers—and then set them loose on a most unlikely target.

The first expansion of the year, *Rise of Shadows*, would focus on the League of E.V.I.L. and their clumsy attempt to steal Dalaran, the flying city. And just to be clear, that wasn't a typo. They weren't trying to steal the goods *inside* Dalaran; they wanted the whole city. As Rafaam put it, "We'll take Dalaran for *all* that it's got!"

But to get it, they'd have to fight the Kirin Tor, the most powerful mages in Azeroth.

Sure, Rafaam hadn't quite figured out how to actually pull off the daring heist, but everybody knows details are for lackeys. Fortunately, *Rise of Shadows* would have plenty of those.

LEFT
Arthur Bozonnet

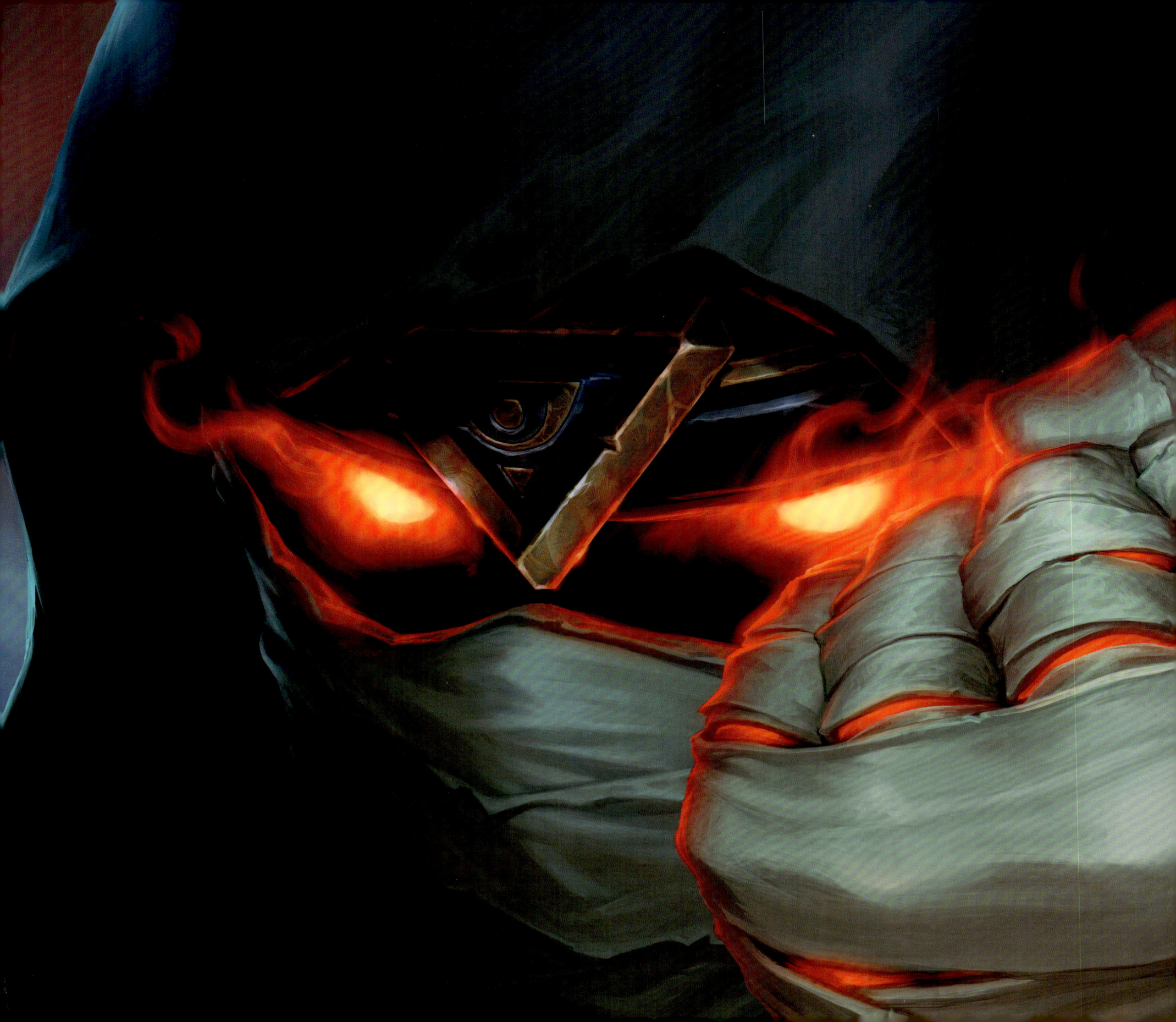

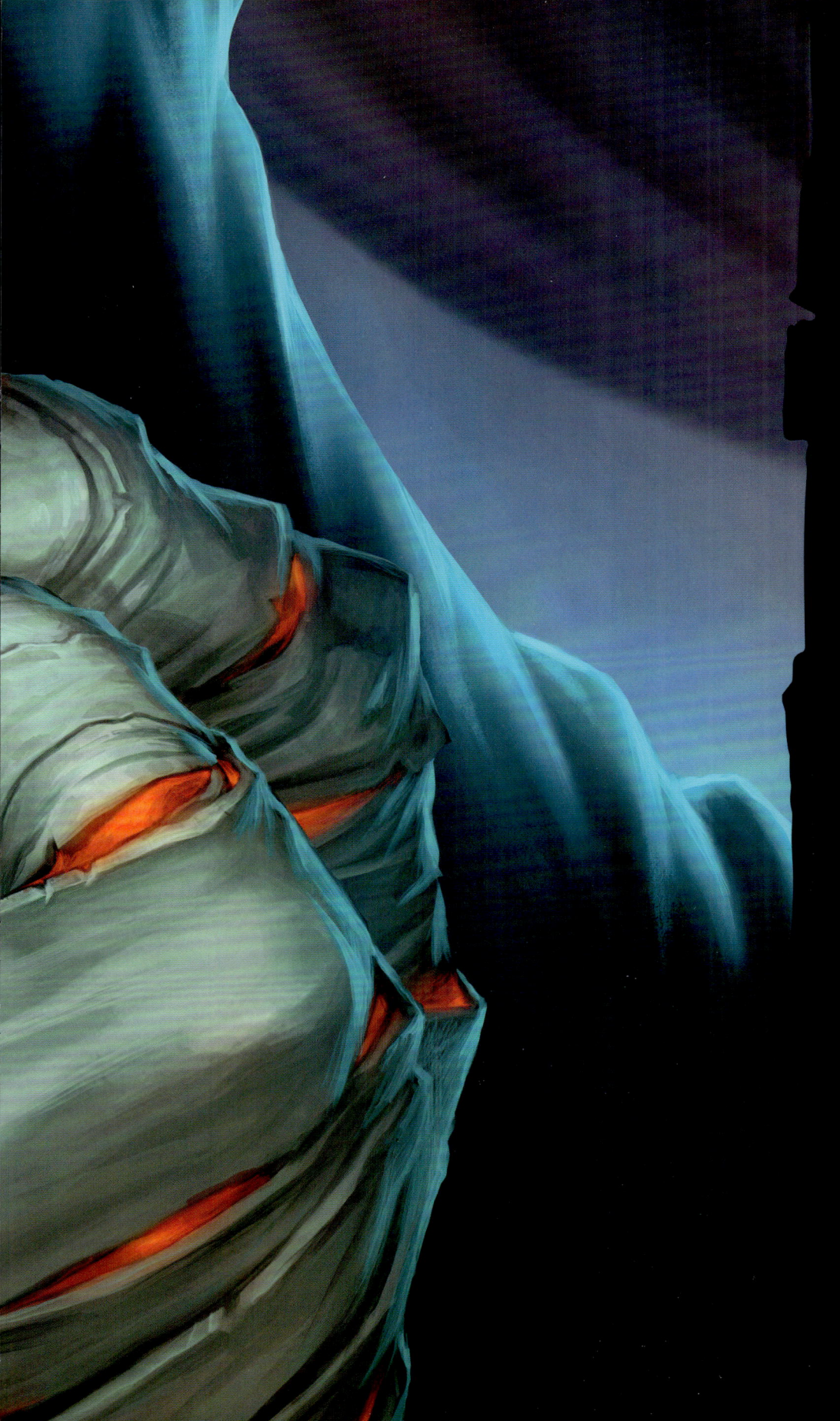

> *You see,
> I have a devious plan that
> requires a demonstrative fist.
> And each of you will have
> your dreams come true
> as a fiendish finger of this!*
>
> —RAFAAM

LEFT
David Kegg

RIGHT
David Kegg
and Maximilian Degen

*We've been given black eyes by the good guys.
But that's about to change! Those meddlesome mortals who've mucked up our missions will finally feel some of our pain!*

—RAFAAM

RIGHT
Peter Stapleton

We'll come together so we can dismantle!

–Hagatha

LEFT
Maximilian Degen

FOLLOWING SPREAD
Peter Stapleton

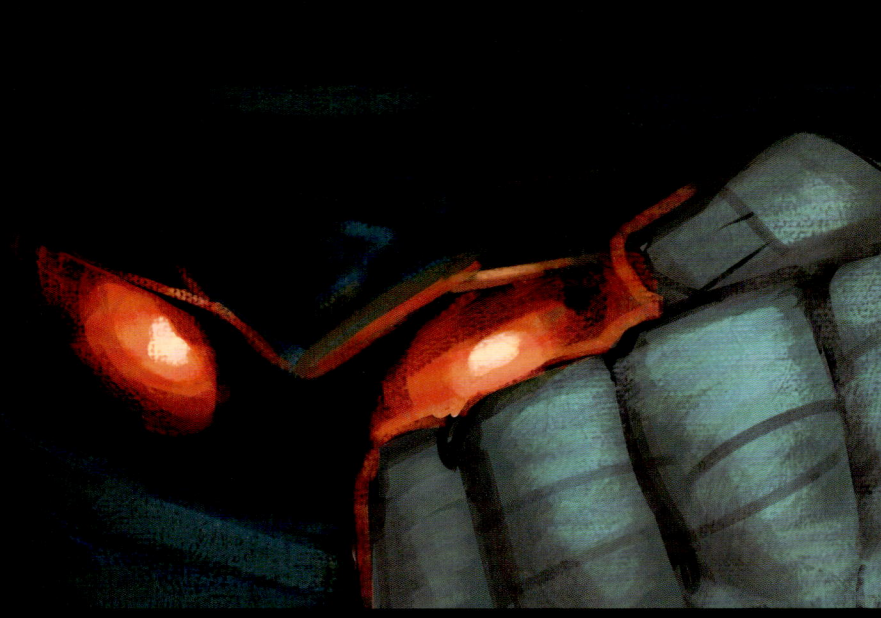

THIS SPREAD
Ludo Lullabi and Sam Nielson

THIS PAGE
Ben Thompson and Chris Hayes

OPPOSITE
Charlène Le Scanff

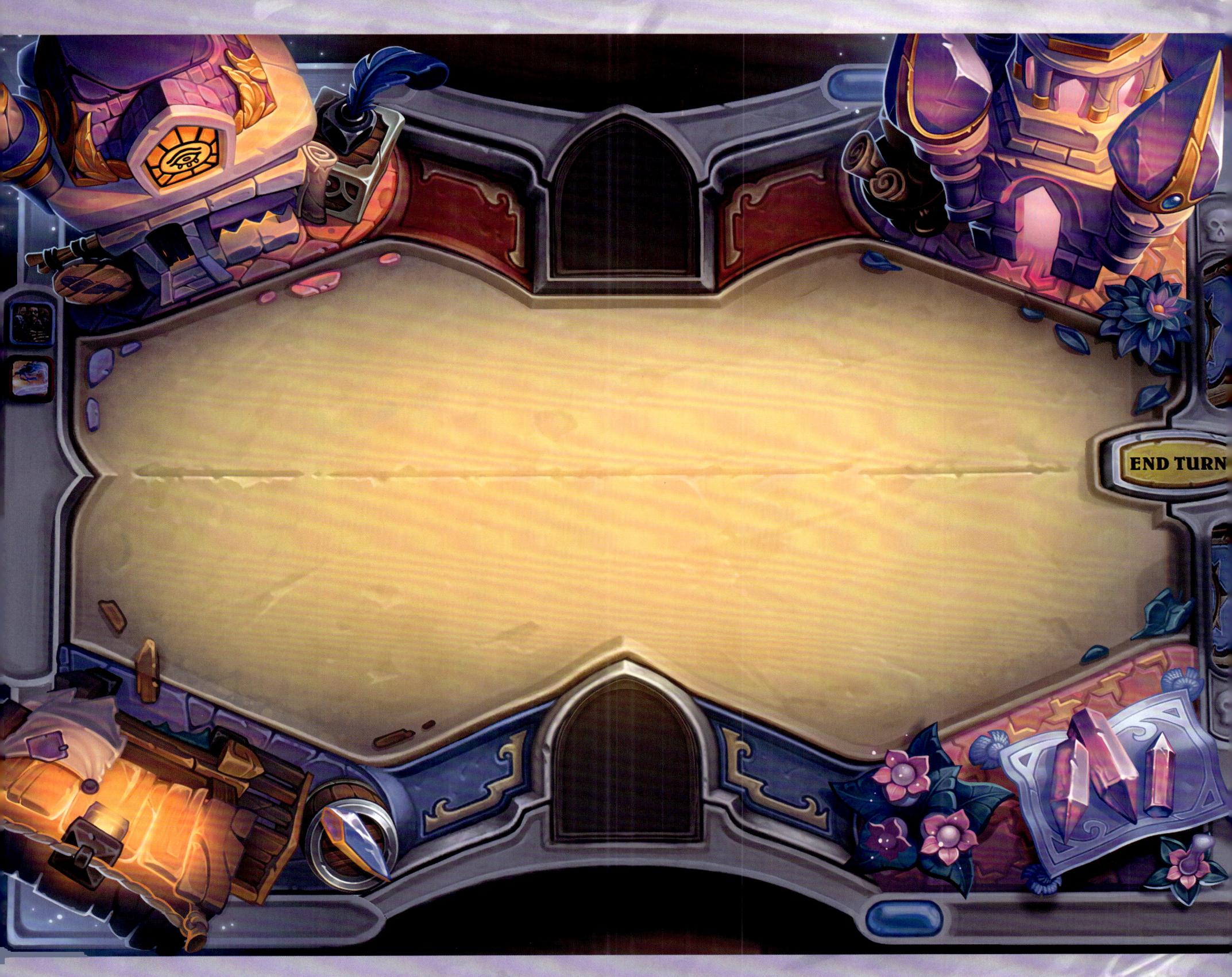

LACKEYS, ASSEMBLE!

The **Lackey** was one of the most impactful new features of the expansion. Lackeys weren't collectible cards; instead, they were generated from other cards. These five small minions—all one-mana, one-health, one-attack minions—had simple Battlecries with a variety of small effects, just enough to eke out advantages at opportune moments.

It wasn't the first time small, generated cards had been used in *Hearthstone*, and that meant the design team had already learned plenty of lessons about how they worked. Finding a name for them proved unexpectedly hard, though.

"The most obvious name was 'Minion,'" said principal designer Peter Whalen, "but that was already what we called *every single playable character* in the game. I can't even remember how many different name ideas we went through before we settled on 'Lackey.'"

The feature had its roots in the **Spare Parts** cards from the first full expansion, *Goblins vs Gnomes*. To differentiate them in early prototypes, designers tried making them more powerful and costly, but it ended up backfiring. "We thought it would be fine to make them two- or three-mana units and spells, with different options relating to each villain, but they were way too strong," Whalen said.

In the end, shrinking them back down to their one-mana mechanized cousins balanced them out. And they were a type that was carried through the entire Year of the Dragon. New Lackeys were added in the next two expansions, expanding the range of power they could unleash.

LEFT
Charlène Le Scanff

RIGHT
Jason Kim

OPPOSITE
Josh Harris

THIS SPREAD
Charlène Le Scanff

THIS SPREAD
Josh Harris

SHADOW MASK
MOUTH = BANDAGE SPACE

THE USUAL SUSPECTS

The class design process, which had been taken to new heights in *The Boomsday Project* only a few months earlier, had demonstrated the power of creating distinct gameplay and visual boundaries between classes early in the design process. In that expansion, each class was helmed by a different scientist and situated in different laboratories. In the next expansion, *Rastakhan's Rumble*, each class was drawn from a different troll tribe and was represented by a unique champion and the Loa they served.

But *Rise of Shadows* wasn't just the next expansion; it was the first act of a yearlong narrative. The team not only needed to solve gameplay for one set—they had to lay the foundation for two more. There were countless ideas for how to make each release feel special.

"The team discussed having different villains show up for each expansion. The team discussed having the *same* villains show up in each set with new cards and new effects," said senior narrative designer Matthew London. "In the end, they found a very fun solution."

The nine different *Hearthstone* classes would be separated into four heroes and five villains. Only the yearlong villains were introduced in the first set, but the hero classes would find plenty of allies in the noble protectors of Dalaran as the yearlong campaign unfolded.

"The team had to look ahead to make sure the heroes would have their own opportunity to shine in the next expansion, but they also needed those classes to have some heavy hitters in this one," said senior art manager Jeremy Cranford.

THESE PAGES
Jomaro Kindred

FOLLOWING SPREAD
LEFT
Ludo Lullabi
RIGHT
Alex Horley

PATCHWORK FACELESS

Khadgar and Kalecgos gave the mage class boosts in value and just plain "big" spells and minions; Vereesa Windrunner and her legendary bow Thori'dal unleashed some magical firepower for hunters; Nozari and Commander Rhyssa anchored paladins with some surprising secrets and comeback mechanics; and the druids of Dalaran rallied behind Keeper Stalladris and Lucentbark.

It took some discussion to decide exactly which classes should be paired with which villains. Hagatha and Dr. Boom had been hero cards for the shaman and warrior classes, respectively, so there wasn't much debate there. King Togwaggle was the ruler of a sneaky empire of kobold thieves, so the rogue class seemed like a good fit for him. Madame Lazul had a sinister connection with the Old Gods and the Void, so it made sense to consider her a priest (a Shadow priest, that is).

Arch-Villain Rafaam could have worked in any class—"I like your class . . . I think I will *take* it!"—but his Battlecry effect was too much fun to play in a warlock deck to put him anywhere else.

The villain classes offered an opportunity to tap into some homegrown nostalgia. Arch-Villain Rafaam's Battlecry called back to the effect of the Golden Monkey in *League of Explorers*. As returning characters, the League of E.V.I.L. brought with them fan-favorite mechanics from expansions past. Heistbaron Togwaggle, leading up a kobold-focused rogues' gallery, brought back the "unidentified" school of cards with Unidentified Contract, which would only reveal its randomized effect once it was drawn from the deck. Blastmaster Boom, heading up the mechanized warrior class once again, dispensed bombs aplenty, both on the board and in his opponent's deck, twinning two mechanics from *Goblins vs Gnomes* and *The Boomsday Project*.

As far as the visual approach was concerned, the villains needed a fresh makeover to reflect their new alliance. "Our first concepts showed all of the villains decked out in red," said senior art manager Jeremy Cranford, "but eventually we settled on something a little more unexpected."

The final look of the League of E.V.I.L. was wrought in violet, particularly the fashionable hooded cloak the five leaders wore. Not only did it feel better across all the different heroes, but it played well with the arcane-hued locations within Dalaran.

"Each villain had their own role in the heist," said senior narrative designer Valerie Chu. "Each of them took down a specific part of the city. Whether they did it well was something else entirely."

LEFT
Jomaro Kindred

OPPOSITE
Jim Nelson

THIS SPREAD
Ludo Lullabi

MORE FIREPOWER!

If the villain classes were getting powerful crime lords, lackeys, and bombastic weapons to use, the remaining classes needed something special with which to fight back. The new keyword, **Twinspell**, was only accessible to the four hero classes and reflected the magical prowess of the defenders of Dalaran.

Designers tried many magic-oriented features before arriving at Twinspell. An early idea that showed promise was magic wands: special weapons that could be equipped by the four hero classes. Instead of attacking with the hero like most other weapons, they would play more like targeted Hero Powers.

"A 'wand of fireball' could shoot the **Fireball** spell at any target you wanted, and then it would lose one durability," said senior designer Chadd Nervig.

Unfortunately, this approach never felt fully intuitive. Adopting the interface of a weapon just didn't feel right in playtests. The next iteration tried the same effect, but as a spell card with multiple uses. It had worked pretty well for the **Echo** keyword in the previous year, but those tended to be low-cost cards, and designers were playing with some much more powerful effects now.

Finally, designers prototyped a spell that allowed for multiple charges and wouldn't disappear at the end of the turn like Echo did. It felt immediately comfortable to players, and so the final Twinspell effect was locked in with a simple description: *Can be cast twice*.

"We took the parts of the idea we liked, we simplified it, and we boiled it down to a keyword that was easy to understand," Nervig said. "When you can get 95 percent of the idea into a format that's only half as complex as the initial pitch, that's called a win."

When the dust settled in Dalaran, the mayhem had left the city's defenders scattered and overrun. The Kirin Tor had been defeated. Against all odds and logic, the League of E.V.I.L. had seized control of Dalaran.

Unless some heroes stepped in soon, the world would be doomed.

THIS PAGE
Blastmaster Boom
Matt Dixon

OPPOSITE
Madame Lazul
J. Axer

OPPOSITE
Arch-Villain Rafaam
Alex Horley

RIGHT
Heistbaron Togwaggle
Ludo Lullabi
& Konstantin Turovec

OPPOSITE
Swampqueen Hagatha
Alex Horley

RIGHT
Drustvar Horror
Alex Horley

ABOVE
Wyvern
Ludo Lullabi
& Konstantin Turovec

ABOVE
Kalecgos
Chris Rahn

ABOVE
Bronze Herald
Alex Horley

ABOVE
Bronze Dragon
Alex Horley

OPPOSITE
Rapid Fire
Ludo Lullabi
& Konstantin Turovec

RIGHT
Vereesa Windrunner
James Ryman

ABOVE
Ethereal Lackey
Rafael Zanchetin

ABOVE
Dalaran Crusader
James Ryman

OPPOSITE
Archmage Vargoth
James Ryman

OPPOSITE
Sunreaver Warmage
Zoltan Boros

ABOVE
Eccentric Scribe
Charlène Le Scanff
Zoltan Boros

ABOVE
Goblin Lackey
Ivan Fomin

ABOVE
Hench-Clan Shadequill
Paul Mafayon

ABOVE
Convincing Infiltrator
Zoltan Boros

ABOVE
Flight Master
Evgeniy Dlinnov

ABOVE
Gryphon
Evgeniy Dlinnov

ABOVE
Walking Fountain
James Ryman

ABOVE
Ursatron
Zoltan Boros

ABOVE
Clockwork Goblin
A.J. Nazzaro

ABOVE
Vicious Scraphound
Dave Allsop

OPPOSITTE
Improve Morale
Matt Dixon

RIGHT
Ol' Barkeye
Rodrigo Camilo

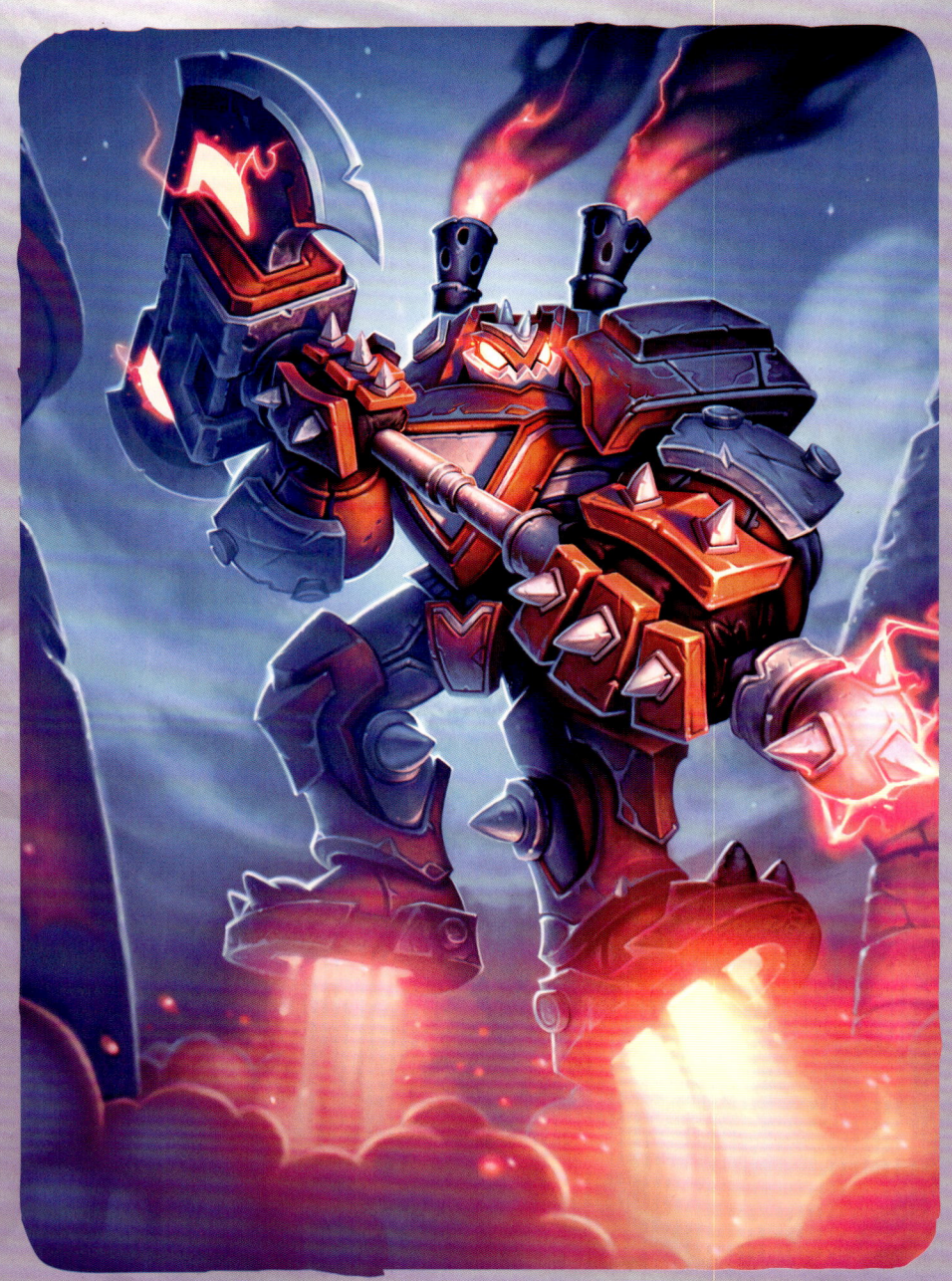

ABOVE
The Boom Reaver
Jerry Mascho

ABOVE
The Boom Reaver Minion
James Ryman

ABOVE
Murloc Muncher
Nicola Saviori

ABOVE
Oblivitron
Zoltan Boros

ABOVE
Safeguard
Ludo Lullabi & Konstantin Turovec

ABOVE
Vault Safe
Ludo Lullabi & Konstantin Turovec

ABOVE
Togwaggle's Scheme
Konstantin Turovec

ABOVE
Soldier of Fortune
Rafael Zanchetin

ABOVE
Evil Cable Rat
Jim Nelson

ABOVE
Muckmorpher
Alex Dixon

ABOVE
Moragg
Mike Sass

ABOVE
Hecklebot
Matt Dixon

TOP LEFT
Unidentified Contract
Akkapoj Thawornsathitwong

BOTTOM LEFT
Recruitment Contract
Akkapoj Thawornsathitwong

TOP RIGHT
Lucrative Contract
Akkapoj Thawornsathitwong

BOTTOM RIGHT
Turncoat Contract
Akkapoj Thawornsathitwong

TOP LEFT
Tunnel Blaster
Ivan Fomin

TOP RIGHT
Tak Nozwhisker
Rafael Zanchetin

BOTTOM LEFT
Recurring Villain
Matt Dixon

BOTTOM RIGHT
Kobold Lackey
Ivan Fomin

ABOVE
Scargil
Alex Horley

ABOVE
Hench-Clan Hogsteed
Matt Dixon

ABOVE
Underbelly Angler
Jim Nelson

ABOVE
Catrina Muerte
Mike Sass

ABOVE
Crystal Dryad
Ludo Lullabi & Konstantin Turovec

ABOVE
Violet Spellsword
Luke Mancini

ABOVE
Lucentbark
Steven Prescott

ABOVE
Mana Reservoir
Jakub Kasper

OPPOSITE
Portal Overfiend
Nicola Saviori

RIGHT
Portal Keeper
Nicola Saviori

3

SAVIORS OF ULDUM

As E.V.I.L. descends from the skies, the world cries out: "How will we survive?"

—Adventuring Song

SAVIORS OF ULDUM SHOW LEADERSHIP

DIRECTOR JERAMIAH JOHNSON
PRODUCER JEFF WONG
ART LEAD WILL MURAI / SAM NIELSON

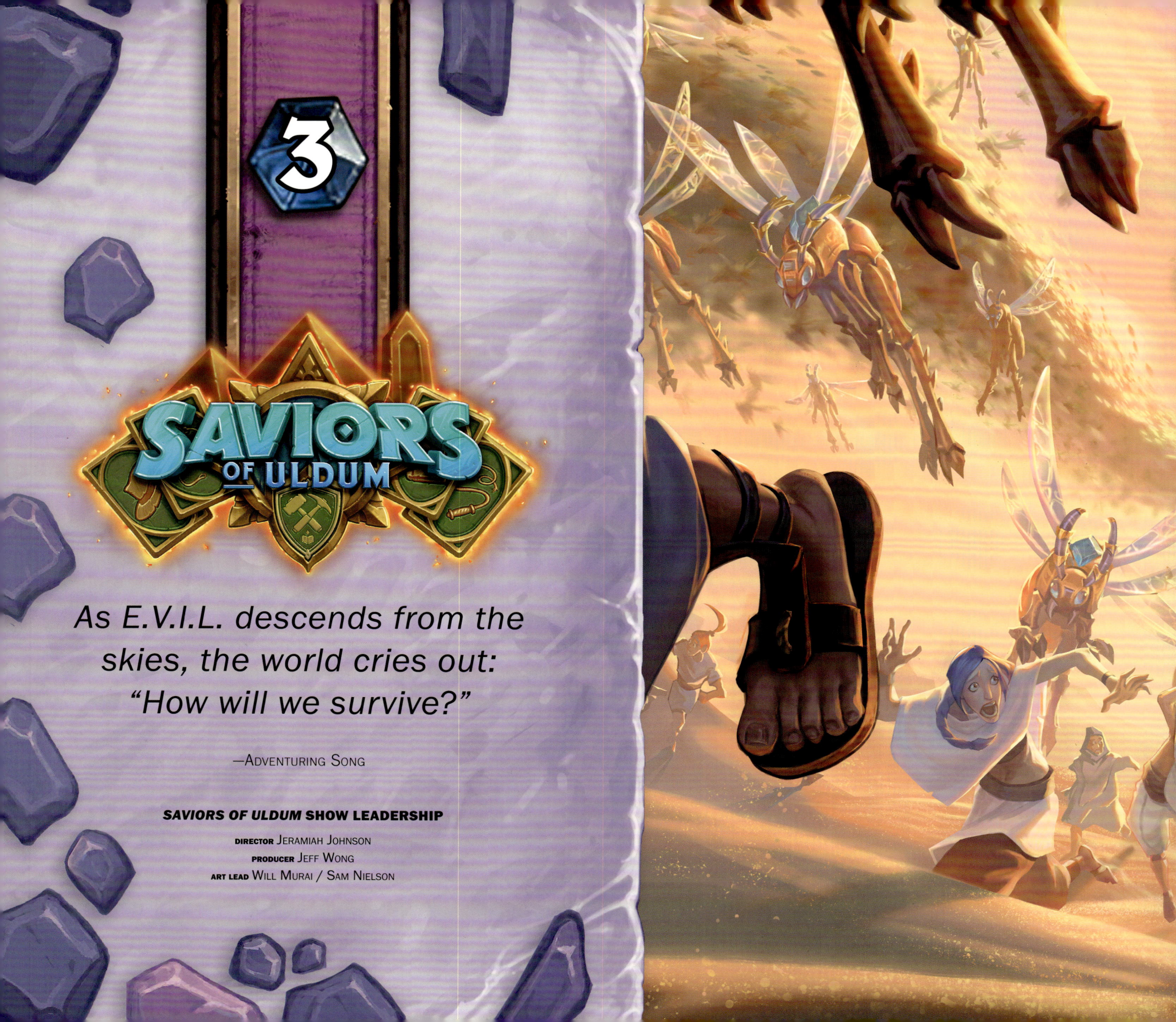

HOLDING OUT FOR A HERO

Improbably, the League of E.V.I.L. somehow succeeded in their heist. They defeated the Kirin Tor and stole the entire city of Dalaran. Next, they arrived in the mysterious ruins of Uldum, the ancient desert facility built by the titans, seeking to claim the deadly secrets within.

Fortunately, it wasn't exactly a clean getaway. Dr. Boom is a terrible pilot, and Dalaran's reckless flight across Azeroth left a trail anyone could follow.

Enter the League of Explorers. Once news spread about Dalaran's bumpy joyride, the good guys leapt into action, chasing the floating city all the way to the southern deserts of Kalimdor. The brave Brann Bronzebeard, the scholarly Elise Starseeker, the stalwart Sir Finley Mrrgglton, and the vaguely competent Reno Jackson were all willing to lay their lives on the line to save the world.

Moreover, the League of Explorers had a personal bone to pick: Rafaam had stolen their acronym, LoE! The League of Explorers would never allow the League of E.V.I.L to snatch one of their most profitable trademarks.

PREVIOUS PAGE
MAR Studio

RIGHT
MAR Studio

But the LoE leaders did not come alone. Junior members of the League of Explorers volunteered for this dangerous mission, hoping to prove themselves and protect one of the most ancient and storied locations in the world. The Uldum locals also joined in the fight, eager to repel the invaders.

Even so, they scarcely could have imagined the threats that awaited them in Uldum. The League of E.V.I.L. had already plundered most of the ruins, finding countless powerful artifacts. Even worse, they had unleashed five deadly plagues that had been sealed beneath the sands long ago.

Like it or not, the League of Explorers was the world's only hope. To stop the League of E.V.I.L., they would need to ~~steal~~ collect whatever artifacts remained hidden in the tombs beneath Uldum, contain the disasters spreading across the land, and then destroy five Plague Lords.

Easy, right?

> *The shadows are rising again, darker than they've ever been . . .*
>
> —Adventuring Song

RIGHT
MAR Studio

They grab their whips and fedoras ... these legends of the past know exactly what to do!

—Adventuring Song

LEFT
MAR Studio

*Out of the Hall of Explorers . . .
and up from the dusty tombs . . .*

—Adventuring Song

RIGHT
MAR Studio

FOLLOWING SPREAD
Peter Stapleton

THESE PAGES
Ludo Lullabi & Sam Nielson

THIS PAGE
Ben Thompson

OPPOSITE
Josh Harris

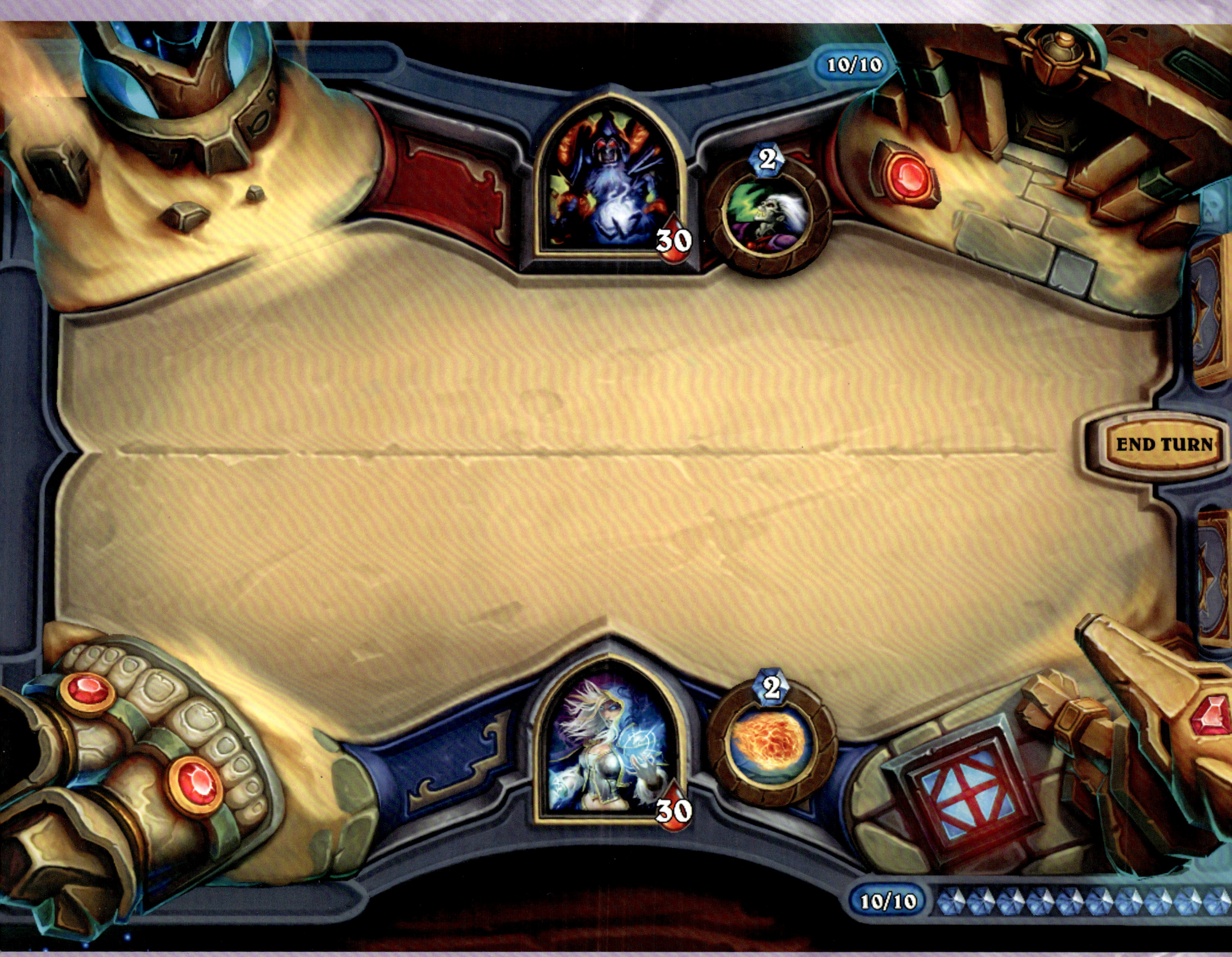

SECRETS BENEATH THE SANDS

The first Year of the Dragon expansion took place in Dalaran, a floating city that *World of Warcraft* players have explored for more than a decade. Since the location was embedded so deeply in the minds of the audience, there was little room for interpretation. The citadels had a specific look. So did the plaza near the fountain. So did the secret sewers beneath the streets. And so on.

In Uldum, the opposite was true. It had been an important location in the *World of Warcraft: Cataclysm* expansion, but it was also a wide-open desert instead of a contained city. Players who had explored every inch of Uldum and made runs to the Throne of the Four Winds every weekend for two years in search of that pesky mount would know better than anyone that *anything* could be hidden beneath the sands. Players had only seen a few secrets. Countless others were yet to be found—and the *Hearthstone* designers intended to exploit that in the second Year of the Dragon expansion, *Saviors of Uldum*.

"The designers really wanted to make sure environments reflected the stories they wanted to tell," said senior art manager Jeremy Cranford. "Especially since they were bringing back legendary quests."

The **Quest** card had been introduced in *Journey to Un'Goro* and had been used then to illustrate the different kinds of dangers the Explorers would find in the jungle-filled crater. In the second act of the Year of the Dragon's yearlong narrative, Quest cards offered a chance to show what each character was doing in the struggle between good and evil.

ABOVE
Charlène Le Scanff

TOP RIGHT
Josh Harris

OPPOSITE
Jerry Mascho

SHADOOF

CATTAIL

PAPYRUS

OASIS CASCADE

"All of our minions primarily show characters. Most of our spells show a character performing an action," said senior designer Chadd Nervig. "*Journey to Un'Goro* showed us how this kind of card should show landscapes, so we wanted to take advantage of that."

In *Saviors of Uldum*, the League of E.V.I.L.'s villains were breaking into the most volatile parts of the desert to unleash the devastating power within, sowing chaos across the land. Meanwhile, the Explorers rushed to combat them and contain the damage. Against this backdrop, the Quest card **Worthy Expedition** shows a member of the League of Explorers surveying a calm oasis; **Corrupt the Waters** shows Hagatha raising an army of murlocs from its waters. **Hack the System** shows Dr. Boom breaking titan machines deep beneath Uldum's ruins; **Unseal the Vault** reveals Brann Bronzebeard's expedition into an undiscovered titan cache.

"Sometimes the team wants to focus on a character or creature; other times they ask for a more narrative composition," said illustrator Ludo Lullabi. "In the first case, I focus on highlighting the subject in an interesting pose. In the second case, I treat it like I'm making a comic; I imagine the scene as a whole, and I try to show the context of the situation."

Back in *Journey to Un'Goro*, when a player completed their Quest, it often felt like the game was over. If the opponent did not have a way to end the game immediately, the Quest reward could snowball out of control.

"This time we wanted the Quests to be slightly easier to achieve and to have a more gradual power boost," said principal designer Peter Whalen. "If you're playing against it, you know you have six or seven turns to find victory, not two or three turns. It's not very fun to feel like you're playing a hopeless game."

THIS PAGE
Charlène Le Scanff

OPPOSITE
Ludo Lullabi

UNANTICIPATED POWER

The class split between heroes and villains was still in effect. The League of E.V.I.L. had been the focus in the last expansion, so now it was the heroes' time to shine. **Elise the Enlightened** represented the druid class as a legendary, **Dinotamer Brann** rode a *T. rex* into battle for the hunter class, **Sir Finley of the Sands** braved the mummies of Uldum for the paladin class, and **Reno the Relicologist** unleashed a barrage of spells as a . . . mage?

Excuse me? Since when is Reno Jackson a mage?

"We were thinking about Reno as a rogue-class character, but he got pushed out by Togwaggle," laughed senior designer Liv Breeden. "But he's such a goof, we realized we could play a different side of him. He's not a trained mage, but he's stolen so many magic wands that he taped them all together. Now he has a magical Gatling gun, basically. In his mind, it's close enough to being a mage."

What sort of spells would come out when he spun up his makeshift cannon? What would they hit? Reno didn't know (and didn't care), but it sure blew things up real nice.

And there were other ways to give players excessive power: huge, powerful spells. The villain classes got spells themed after the hidden plagues of Uldum, such as **Plague of Death** and **Plague of Wrath**, which could upend the entire board state for both players. "Plagues can't be controlled, after all," said principal designer Peter Whalen.

All classes had unique big spells. **Tip the Scales**, a paladin spell, floods the board with murlocs, and **Puzzle Box of Yogg-Saron**, a mage spell, spins a roulette wheel of death and destruction with unpredictable results.

"The spells of this expansion were powerful enough to actually break the interface a bit," said lead UI/UX designer Max Ma.

Earthquake is a shaman spell that unleashes five damage across the board, and then two damage more. Any cards that had tricky **Deathrattles**, especially those that spawned small little tokens, would find those being wiped out, too. Dozens of minions could die in a single turn, transforming the history bar on the left side of the game board into an unreadable mess.

"But that's actually a good thing, if it doesn't happen too often," Ma explained. "It's been a philosophical pillar of the game since the beginning: when the player breaks their own game with an awesome play, they actually feel good about it. As long as the game still functions, it's satisfying to feel like you've made a play the designers never anticipated."

But a new keyword proved to be one of the most impactful new mechanics: **Reborn**. Uldum is a land filled with restless mummies rising from their dusty tombs, and the team played with several ideas for how to use them in gameplay.

It turned out to be a simple-to-understand mechanic ("Resurrects with 1 Health the first time it dies."), and it was different enough from the **Deathrattle** keyword that the designers didn't have to worry much about overlap. Smaller minions with Reborn could become lingering annoyances to your opponent, while bigger Reborn cards could be huge threats that your opponent would have to deal with twice.

"The art team and the engineering team made the Reborn effect look so good on the board," said Whalen. "If it wasn't clear what the keyword meant the first time you saw it, the effect taught you everything you needed to know."

There was one important limitation when it came to the art and illustrations for *Saviors of Uldum*. The League of Explorers and the League of E.V.I.L. could not go toe to toe quite yet. For this expansion, the second act of a yearlong narrative, the Explorers needed to save the world by stopping the plagues rather than by confronting their rivals.

This meant the chaos sown in Uldum was just a distraction so the League of E.V.I.L. could escape to pursue its true prize. While the Explorers were busy battling the five Plague Lords, the villains hopped back onto their flying city and sped off.

Rafaam's ultimate objective lay to the north. And despite the Explorers' best efforts, they could not stop him from fleeing with the key to obtaining: the **Plague of Undeath**.

THIS PAGE
Ludo Lullabi

OPPOSITE
Ludo Lullabi
& Konstantin Turovec

THIS PAGE
Charlène Le Scanff

① ② POSSIBLE REBORN?

TOMB OF PYMGY

PYGMY RIDER

PLAGUE OF MUTATION (SHAMAN)

THIS PAGE
Josh Harris

THESE PAGES
Jerry Mascho

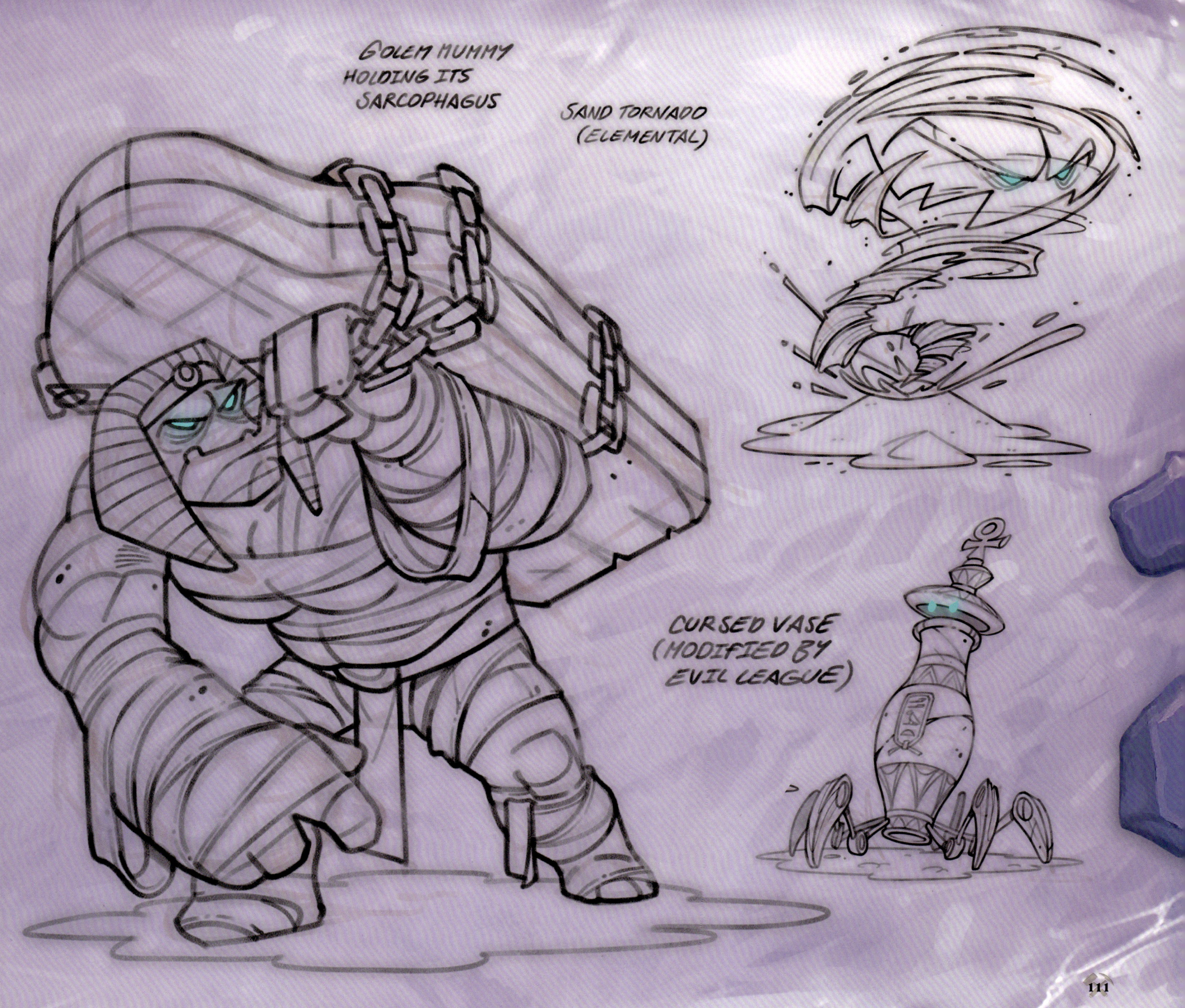

THESE PAGES
Charlène Le Scanff

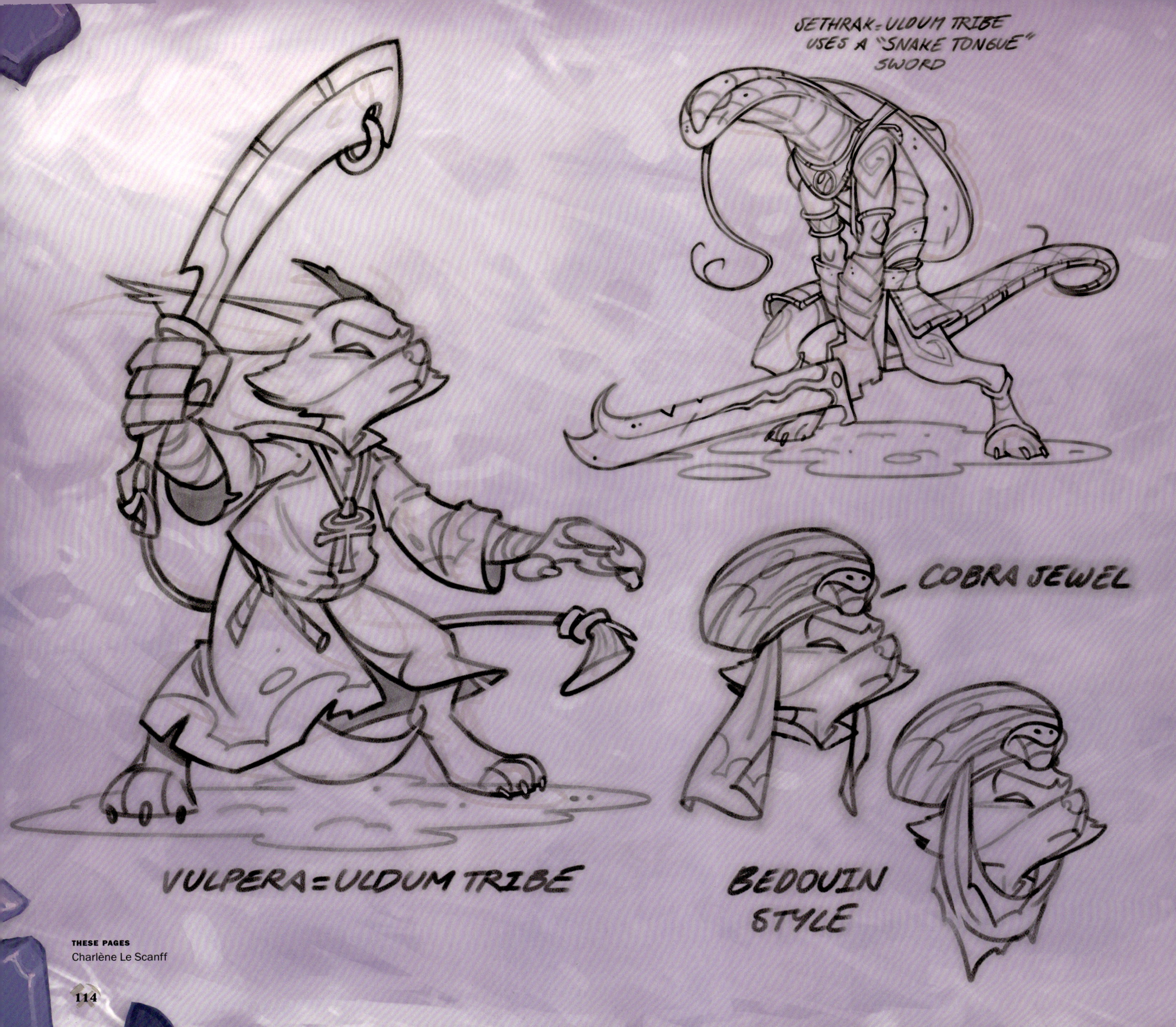

LEFT
Elise the Enlightened
Luke Mancini

OPPOSITE
Dinotamer Brann
Ludo Lullabi
& Konstantin Turovec

OPPOSITE
Sir Finley of the Sands
Matt Dixon

RIGHT
Reno the Relicologist
Eric Braddock

ABOVE
Pressure Plate
Zoltan Boros

OPPOSITTE
Flame Ward
Zoltan Boros

ABOVE
Plague of Flames
Armand Serrano

OPPOSITE
Plague of Death
Zoltan Boros

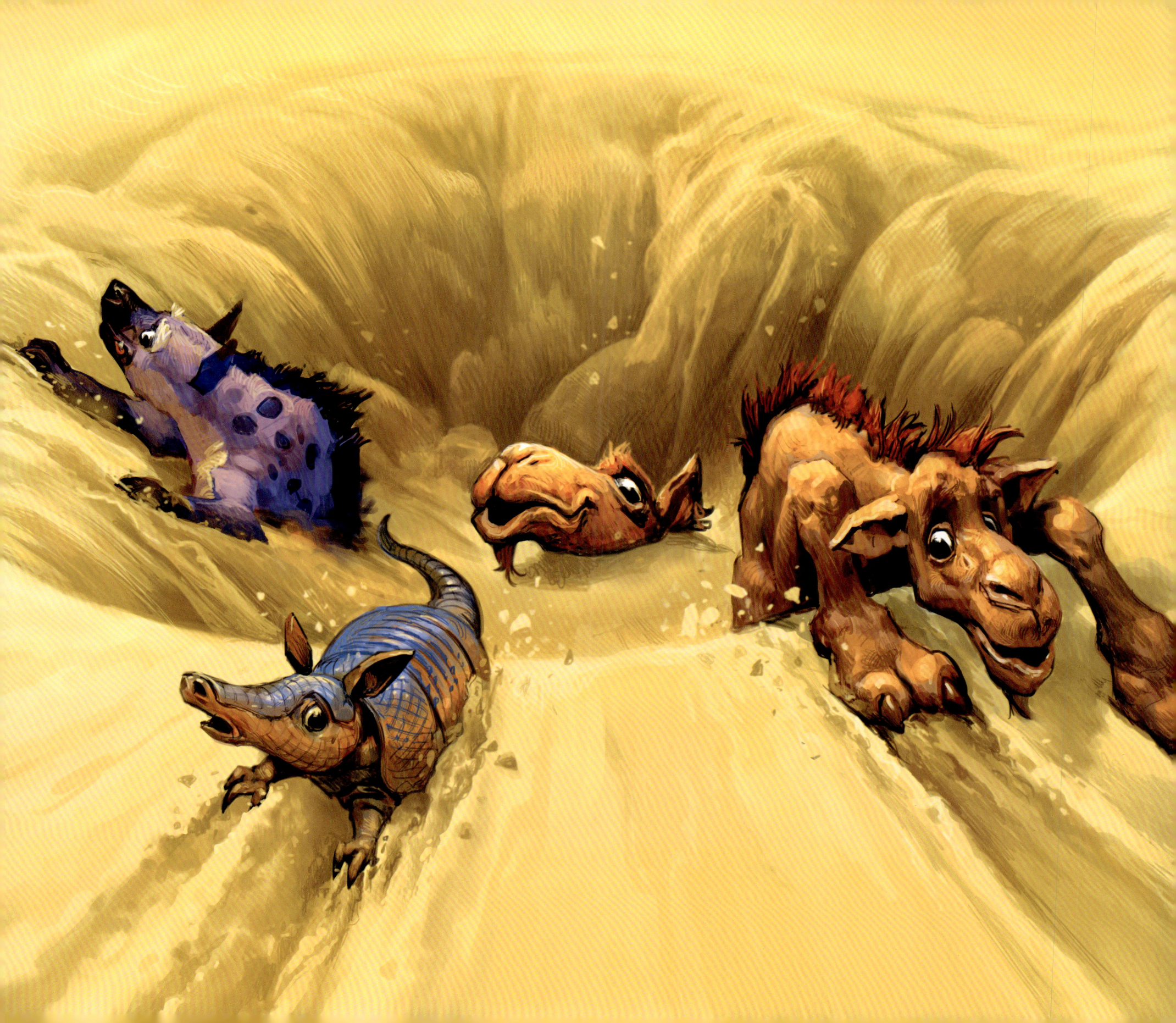

OPPOSITE
Beaming Sidekick
Rafael Zanchetin

TOP LEFT
Anubisath Warbringer
Slawomir Maniak

TOP RIGHT
Dune Sculptor
Servando Lupini

BOTTOM LEFT
Questing Explorer
Maria Trepalina

BOTTOM RIGHT
Bug Collector
Rafael Zanchetin

OPPOSITE
Arcane Flakmage
Ursula Dorada

ABOVE
Infested Goblin
Ludo Lullabi & Konstantin Turovec

ABOVE
Armagedillo
Jaemin Kim

ABOVE
Treant
Ivan Fomin

ABOVE
Garden Gnome
Ivan Fomin

OPPOSITE
Injured Tol'vir
Ludo Lullabi & Konstantin Turovec

ABOVE
Khartut Defender
MAR Studio

ABOVE
Anubashi Defender
James Ryman

ABOVE
Bone Wraith
Steven Prescott

ABOVE
Mogu Fleshshaper
Arthur Gimaldinov

ABOVE
Locust
Rafael Zanchetin

ABOVE
Scarlet Webweaver
Andrew Hou

ABOVE
Wasteland Scorpid
Mauricio Herrera

ABOVE
Bee
Rafael Zanchetin

ABOVE
Swarm of Locusts
Rafael Zanchetin

OPPOSITE
BEEEES!!!
Rafael Zanchetin

ABOVE
Colossus of the Moon
Alex Horley

ABOVE
Crystal Merchant
Ludo Lullabi & Konstantin Turovec

OPPOSITE
Demolisher 3V-11
Phil Saunders

ABOVE
Naga Sand Witch
Mike Sass

ABOVE
Micro Mummy
Matt Dixon

OPPOSITE
Corrupt the Waters
Alex Horley

TOP LEFT
Worthy Expedition
Paul Mafayon

BOTTOM LEFT
Hunter's Pack
Ludo Lullabi & Konstantin Turovec

TOP RIGHT
Canopic Jars
Eugene Dlinnov

BOTTOM RIGHT
Mummy Magic
Eugene Dlinnov

OPPOSITE
Holy Ripple
Anton Zemskov

ABOVE
Neferset Thrasher
Eric Braddock

ABOVE
Highkeeper Ra
James Ryman

ABOVE
King Phaoris
James Ryman

ABOVE
Quicksand Elemental
James Ryman

ABOVE
Siamat
Alex Horley

ABOVE
Ancestral Guardian
César Rosolino

ABOVE
Vessina
James Ryman

ABOVE
Psychopomp
Jim Nelson

OPPOSITE
Penance
James Ryman

TOP
Untapped Potential
Luke Mancini

BOTTOM
Supreme Archaeology
James Ryman

ABOVE
Restless Mummy
Ivan Fomin

ABOVE
Anka, the Buried
Paul Mafayon

ABOVE
Temple Berserker
Jim Nelson

ABOVE
Battrund
Melvin Chan

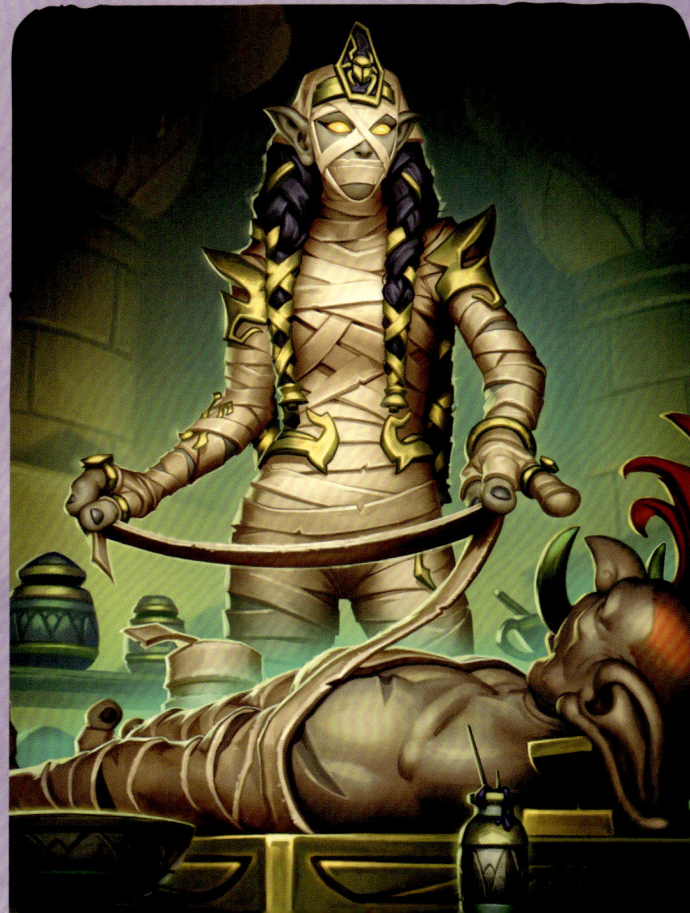

TOP LEFT
Pharaoh Cat
Eva Widermann

TOP RIGHT
Wasteland Assassin
Phroilan Gardner

BOTTOM LEFT
Candletaker
Ivan Fomin

BOTTOM RIGHT
Body Wrapper
Arthur Bozonnet

OPPOSITE
Embalming Ritual
Ivan Fomin

4

DESCENT OF DRAGONS

Dragons take flight above the ice and snow, high in the sky where the cold wind blows!

—Adventuring Song

DESCENT OF DRAGONS SHOW LEADERSHIP

DIRECTOR Jeramiah Johnson
PRODUCER Taka Yasuda
ART LEAD Will Murai / Sam Nielson

DRAGONS!

There have been one-word hooks in *Hearthstone* expansions before. *Journey to Un'Goro*'s pitch was simple: "Dinosaurs!" *Rastakhan's Rumble*? "Trolls!"

The pitch for *Descent of Dragons*, the final expansion of 2019, needs no explanation.

But this wasn't just an expansion about dragons. It was the final battle between the League of Explorers and the League of E.V.I.L. It was the culmination of *Hearthstone*'s first yearlong story arc. It was also the return of the linear single-player narrative adventure.

But mostly, it was a dragon expansion. Not *dragons*, plural. *Dragon*, singular.

Hearthstone was finally ready to introduce the biggest and baddest dragon that has ever existed in *Warcraft* lore.

"Deathwing?" you ask? Of course not! We're talking about Galakrond, the inimitable proto-dragon. He's far bigger than a pipsqueak like Deathwing. And he's far more obscure!

The final battle of the Year of the Dragon was a battle for *the* Dragon. Rafaam and the League of E.V.I.L. sought to raise Galakrond from the snowdrifts of Dragonblight and harness his unstoppable power against the entire world. The League of Explorers stood ready to stop him.

And both sides had lined up armies of dragons to help them. The biggest aerial battle in Azeroth's history was about to begin.

PREVIOUS PAGES
MAR Studio

LEFT
MAR Studio

*Good unites against evil they oppose.
They ride and die as the legends grow!*

—Adventuring Song

RIGHT
MAR Studio

We must all choose sides, villains or heroes. There are no sidelines in this combat zone!

—Adventuring Song

LEFT
MAR Studio

THE FIGHT TAKES FLIGHT

The *Hearthstone* team had known they wanted Galakrond in the final expansion of the year for a long, long time. The name of the whole 2019 arc—Year of the Dragon—was even a reference to the terrifying, undead proto-dragon.

From a design standpoint, Galakrond's overwhelming power in the lore was a chance to introduce some game-changing effects into the meta. Much like how the Old Gods had been dominant, table-flipping cards back in their 2016 expansion, Galakrond needed to be feared and anticipated long before he was ever played in a match.

The effect of the Old Gods had taught the design team valuable lessons about how to manage that sort of power. The **C'Thun** card, in particular, was both an inspiration and a cautionary tale. Many players treated C'Thun as the *Hearthstone* version of a nuclear bomb: play him before your opponent does, and you win.

Like C'Thun, Galakrond would be "charged up" over the course of a match. A new keyword, **Invoke**, would ramp up his power gradually. With two Invokes, Galakrond is upgraded with stronger powers. Two more, and he reaches his final form.

But most importantly, Invoke would unleash Galakrond's Hero Power onto the board even before he was played.

"It gave Galakrond a feeling of inevitability," said principal designer Peter Whalen. "With C'Thun, you were playing weak minions to charge him up, and it was very easy to fall behind. Galakrond would have an impact even before he showed up in person. It was one of the trickiest mechanics we ever shipped in *Hearthstone*. If the art team and the engineering team hadn't made it so clear as to what was happening when Invoke triggered, it might not have worked at all."

RIGHT
MAR Studio

Galakrond differed from C'Thun in another big way: he would not have the same effect across all classes. Each of the five villain classes would have their own unique version of Galakrond, complete with unique upgraded Battlecries and Hero Powers. Gameplay effects range from destroying minions to drawing cards to summoning minions, and upgraded versions include Galakrond's claws as a weapon.

All that meant there would have to be a lot of art for Galakrond. Five classes, three upgraded versions each . . . proto-dragons shouldn't be forced to do math like that!

Hearthstone's concept artists drew up many versions of what the different Galakronds should look like, but the team decided to delegate the creation of the final illustrations to a single artist, just to make sure Galakrond's look was consistent.

"We didn't want people to be comparing styles between artists," said senior art manager Jeremy Cranford. "We wanted the contrasts between the different classes and the upgraded versions to speak for themselves."

Illustrator Konstantin Turovec accepted the challenge of bringing them all to life. Not only was Galakrond the biggest dragon in the Warcraft mythos, but he was also one of the most unusual.

"Huge arms with wings, small *T. rex* hands, large mouth, spikes all over the body, very long tail," Turovec said. "It was hard to paint Galakrond."

RIGHT
MAR Studio

*Skies fill with trauma
in all of this drama,
portending an impending end!
Crash down!
It's dragons in dragons' descent!*

—Adventuring Song

LEFT
MAR Studio

The first version Turovec tried was for the priest class: **Galakrond, the Unspeakable**. Its Void-influenced corruption offered a special challenge, especially in the upgraded illustrations.

"The three different versions had to look distinctive," Turovec said. "I tried to show the inner power of the dragon in each. Corruption has specific and memorable details like orange glowing eyes and purple tentacles. Purple was everywhere, even on the background with the dusk sky! But it worked really well. It gave me a good foundation for the other illustrations."

Each class's version of Galakrond showed his increasing power in unique ways. The warrior class gave him more and more mechanized armor from Dr. Boom's workshop; the shaman class showed an elemental cyclone raging around him; the warlock version showed Galakrond practically exploding with fel energy.

"I had to find the special aspect of each class and use it to my advantage," Turovec added.

All of the dragonflights on Azeroth also took part in the battle over Dragonblight. Many classes got prominent dragonflights of their very own—green dragons fought alongside druids and bronze dragons with paladins. Some, though, had to improvise. The priest class, led by Madame Lazul, got some help from the future with **Murozond the Infinite** and the rest of the corrupted Infinite dragonflight. The rogue class, led by Togwaggle, constructed wax dragons from his leftover candles, resulting in the formidably drippy **Waxadred**.

"When I received the request for a wax-covered dragon with a candle on its head, I wondered if I had understood correctly," said illustrator Ludo Lullabi. "I had to be careful not to make him too much of a caricature. He needed to look dangerous enough to face off against other dragons."

RIGHT
MAR Studio

THESE PAGES
Ludo Lullabi & Sam Nielson

THIS PAGE
Ben Thompson

OPPOSITE
Charlène Le Scanff

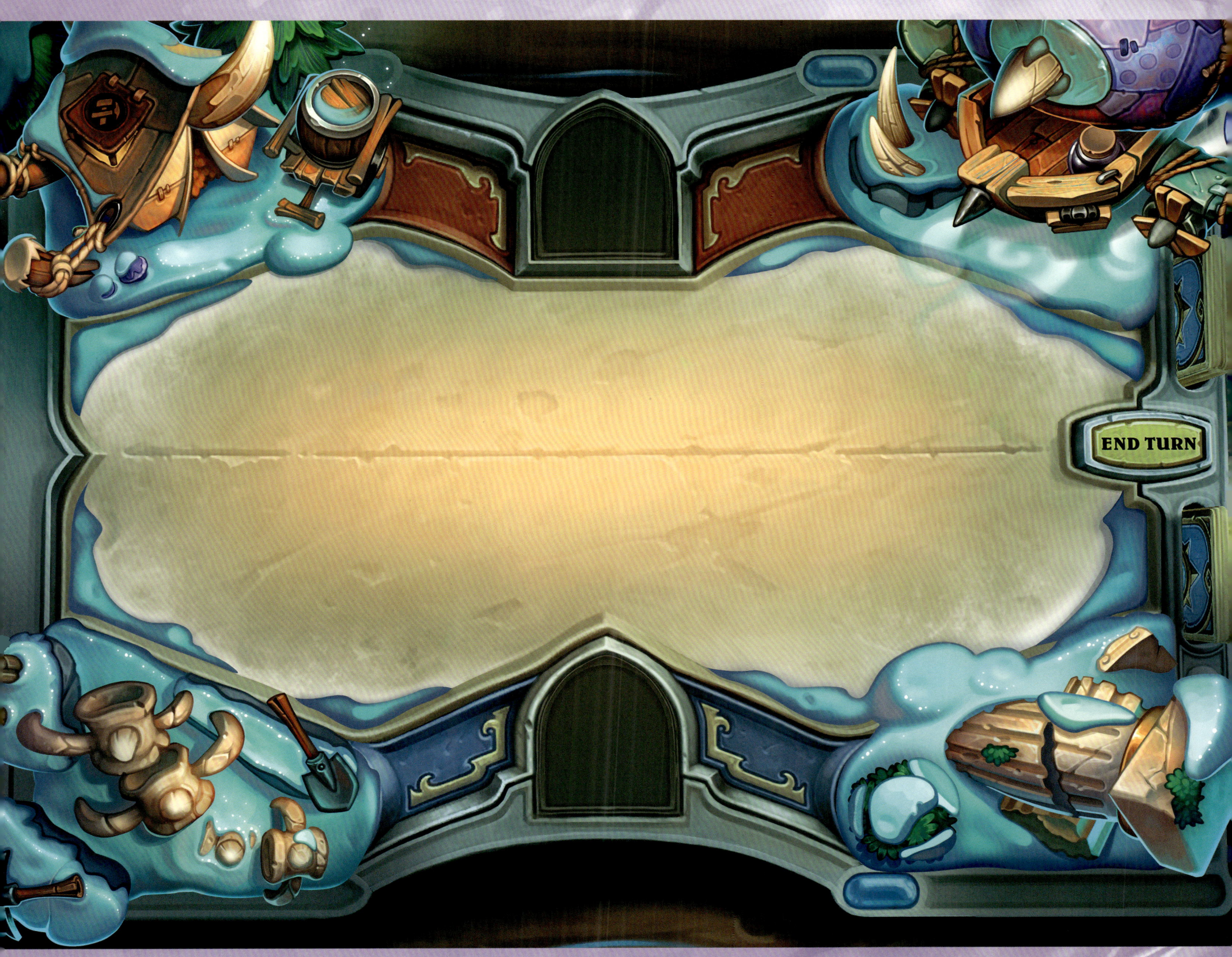

ABOVE
Charlène Le Scanff

RIGHT
Glenn Rane

THESE PAGES
Christopher Hayes

THESE PAGES
Josh Harris

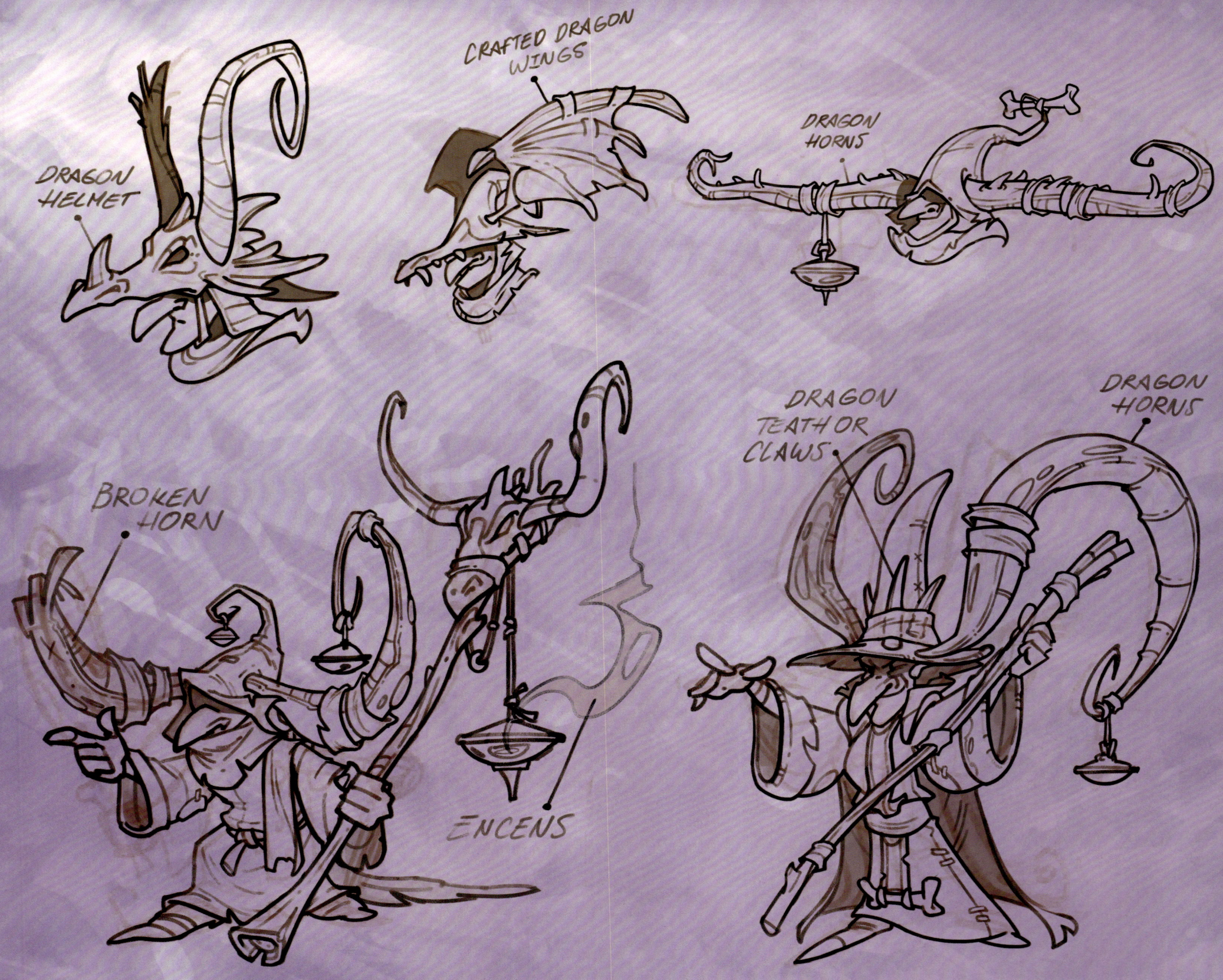

THESE PAGES
Charlène Le Scanff

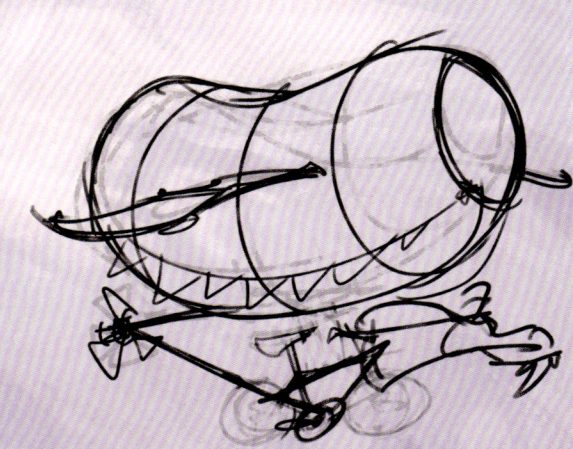

NO PROTO-DRAGON? NO PROBLEM.

While five classes had Galakrond anchoring their new deck archetypes for the expansion, four did not. The heroes of the League of Explorers weren't trying to raise Galakrond, so it didn't make sense for them to Invoke his aid. Instead, they spent some time leveling up for the battle with **Sidequests**.

Just like legendary Quests, Sidequests were one-mana cards that offered a reward for completing certain gameplay objectives. As the name suggests, the rewards were not as dramatic. They were much easier to achieve, and players could put two of them in each deck.

"Sidequests were an old idea for us. I think the first time they were brought up was actually *The Grand Tournament*," said Whalen. "Since we had already reintroduced Quests in the previous expansion, it felt like a good time to finally use the idea."

Though less obviously powerful than a gigantic proto-dragon, Sidequests ended up being a sly answer to the inevitable march toward ultimate, world-shattering power. The mage class, for instance, had **Learn Draconic**, which rewarded you for playing spells.

"You don't need to build a deck around them," said senior designer Liv Breeden. "A mage is going to be playing spells anyway. Spending eight mana on spells can happen very, very fast. Having a 6/6 minion on the board early can be a big deal."

Though this expansion may have the most dragons of any release in *Hearthstone*'s history, barely 20 percent of the collectible cards were dragons. That might seem low, but it actually hits the sweet spot, according to Whalen. "You don't need 90 percent of the cards to be dragons for this to feel like a dragon expansion," he said. "If too many cards are the same type, the set can feel monotonous. *Hearthstone* lives off its variety. The battle over Northrend needed to feel like the two Leagues in conflict, too."

THESE PAGES
Charlène Le Scanff

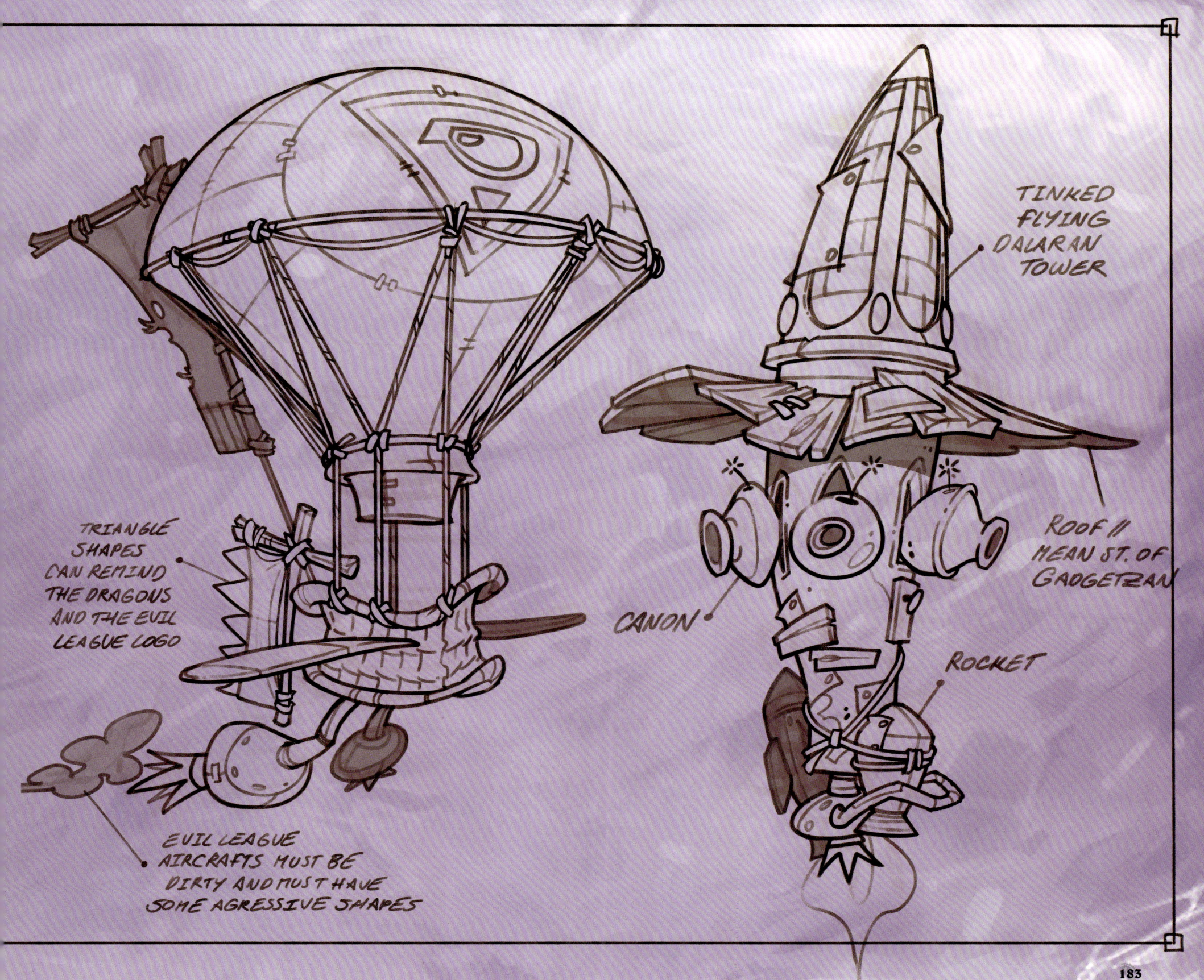

THESE PAGES
Charlène Le Scanff

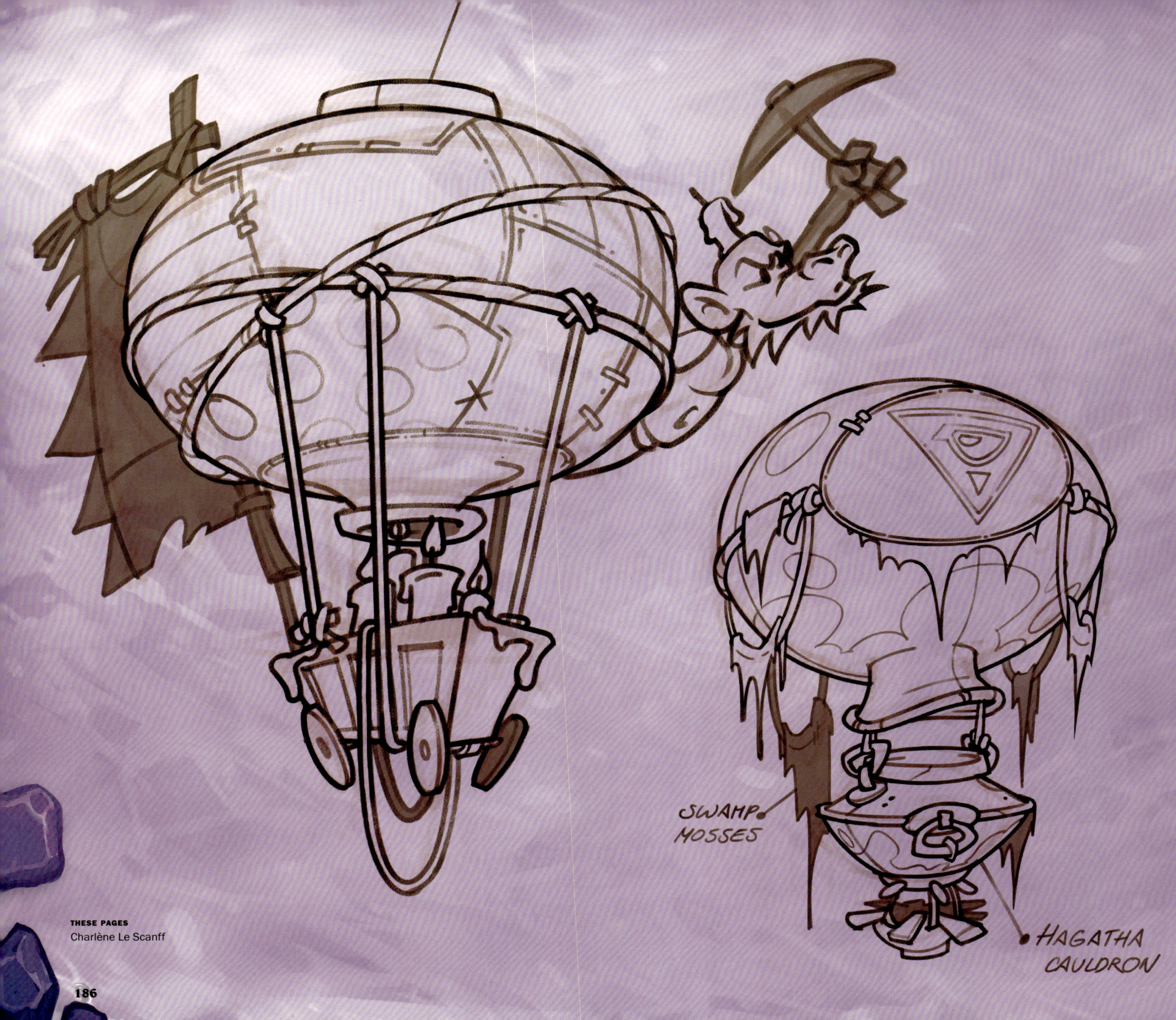

THESE PAGES
Charlène Le Scanff

Indeed, the combined might of the League of Explorers and their allies took flight in diverse ways, and the criminal minions of the League of E.V.I.L. also found novel ways to join them in the clouds.

The design team briefly toyed with mechanical means to reflect the aerial nature of the fighting. One prototype had flying minions able to soar above taunted minions and attack anything they pleased; it was eventually dropped. But the visual idea was too much fun to cut. Giving illustrators the chance to find out how wingless combatants chose to enter a flying battle resulted in dozens of inventive, bizarre, and downright hilarious moments. Some minions used blimps. Others used propeller-driven airships. Some just strapped on wings to their arms and flapped *really* hard. Others jumped onto slingshots and let gravity do the rest. Their illustrations reflected the characters' ingenuity, desperation, and plain old recklessness.

And they needed it all to wage war for the fate of Azeroth. A year's worth of heists, skirmishes, plagues, and schemes all added up to one gigantic battle. The leagues, the dragonflights, and all of their allies and Lackeys would join the fray above the snowcapped peaks of Northrend to claim control over the frozen bones of Galakrond and the power he could wield.

But the ending of this battle was not preordained. To cap off a year of firsts, the *Hearthstone* team would try something they had never attempted before: two separate endings.

OPPOSITE
Jomaro Kindred

BELOW
Ludo Lullabi & Sam Nielson

OPPOSITE
Air Raid
Ivan Fomin

ABOVE
The Amazing Reno (Playable Hero)
Konstantin Turovec

ABOVE
The Amazing Reno (Minion)
Konstantin Turovec

ABOVE
Skyfin
Alex Horley

ABOVE
Azure Explorer
Charlène Le Scanff

OPPOSITE
Big Ol' Whelp
Yare Yue

OPPOSITE
Flik Skyshiv
Matt Dixon

ABOVE
Sky Raider
Ivan Fomin

ABOVE
Goboglide Tech
Matt Dixon

LEFT
Kobold Stickyfinger
Andrew Hou

OPPOSITE
Hoard Pillager
A.J. Nazzaro

ABOVE
Spin 'em Up
Jim Nelson

OPPOSITE
Strength in Numbers
Luke Mancini

ABOVE
Hagatha the Vengeful
Alex Horley

ABOVE
Commander Elise
Luke Mancini

OPPOSITE
Wail of the Shudderwock
Alex Horley

OPPOSITE
Sky Gen'ral Kragg (Unreleased)
James Ryman

ABOVE
Dread Raven
Patrik Björkström

ABOVE
Dragonrider Brann
Konstantin Turovec

ABOVE
Embiggen
Studio Hive

ABOVE
Emerald Explorer
A.J. Nazzaro

OPPOSITE
Twin Tyrant
Mike Sass

ABOVE
Devoted Maniac
Anzka Nguyen

ABOVE
Draconic Imp
A.J. Nazzaro

OPPOSITE
Animated Avalanche
Ludo Lullabi & Konstantin Turovec

LEFT
Dr. Boom
Matt Dixon

TOP LEFT
Puppetmaster Lazul
Matt Dixon

BOTTOM LEFT
Whispers of EVIL
Ivan Fomin

TOP RIGHT
Sir Finley
Matt Dixon

BOTTOM RIGHT
Boom Barrage
Matt Dixon

ABOVE
Nether Drake
Slawomir Maniak

ABOVE
Zzeraku the Warped
Slawomir Maniak

LEFT
Fate Weaver
Andrew Hou

OPPOSITE
Awaken!
Slawomir Maniak

ABOVE
Galakrond, Azeroth's End (Warlock)
Konstantin Turovec

ABOVE
Galakrond, Azeroth's End (Shaman)
Konstantin Turovec

OPPOSITE
Galakrond,
Azeroth's End (Warrior)
Konstantin Turovec

RIGHT
Galakrond,
the Tempest (Shaman)
Konstantin Turovec

LEFT
Galakrond, Azeroth's End (Priest)
Konstantin Turovec

OPPOSITE
Galakrond, Azeroth's End (Rogue)
Konstantin Turovec

ABOVE
Malygos, Aspect of Magic
Ludo Lullabi & Konstantin Turovec

ABOVE
Nozdormu the Timeless
Ludo Lullabi & Konstantin Turovec

ABOVE
Ysera, Unleashed
Ludo Lullabi & Konstantin Turovec

ABOVE
Diving Gryphon
Mike Sass

ABOVE
Dragoncaster
David Kegg

ABOVE
Dragonmaw Poacher
Rafael Zanchetin

ABOVE
Grand Lackey Erkh
James Ryman

ABOVE
Platebreaker
Paul Mafayon

TOP LEFT
Arcane Breath
MAR Studio

TOP RIGHT
Murozond the Infinite
Ludo Lullabi
& Konstatin Turovec

BOTTOM LEFT
Dragonqueen Alexstrasza
Ludo Lullabi
& Konstatin Turovec

BOTTOM RIGHT
Skybarge
Steven Prescott

OPPOSITE
Sathrovarr
Alex Horley

LEFT
Deathwing, Mad Aspect
Ludo Lullabi
& Konstantin Turovec

OPPOSITE
Storm Drake
Anton Zemskov

ABOVE
Troll Batrider
Jim Nelson

ABOVE
Wing Commander
Jim Nelson

OPPOSITE
Scalerider
Rafael Zanchetin

TOP LEFT
Invocation of Frost
Ludo Lullabi & Konstantin Turovec

BOTTOM LEFT
Lightning Breath
Zoltan Boros

TOP RIGHT
Storm's Wrath
Zoltan Boros

BOTTOM RIGHT
Breath of Dreams
James Ryman

OPPOSITE
The Dragonflights
Zoltan Boros

ABOVE
Kronx Dragonhoof
Jerry Mascho

ABOVE
Bandersmosh
Matt Dixon

ABOVE
Camouflaged Dirigible
Matt Dixon

ABOVE
Envoy of Lazul
Jakub Kasper

5

NEW FRONTIERS

Some of these tales are so crazy, they're true.

—Bartender Bob

A YEAR OF STORY

"I don't know. I might be biased, but I really enjoy narrative," laughed senior narrative designer Valerie Chu. "When it's done right, it's like frosting on a cake. Just delicious."

Until the Year of the Dragon, expansions rolled out with a fairly predictable game plan. A cinematic would help announce the new set, the expansion would launch, and then a single-player adventure would often follow shortly thereafter, offering players a chance to have a structured experience with the characters and conflicts depicted in the cards.

Each of the expansions in 2019 would have both of those things. And they would also have so much more.

"The seed was planted long before the Year of the Dragon actually began," said senior missions designer Paul Nguyen. "The villains were gathering together, the good guys were still out there, alive and well, and they would come into conflict once again."

The team brainstormed all sorts of mayhem a yearlong story arc could include and then whittled down the Year of the Dragon into three distinctive acts. The League of E.V.I.L. set things in motion with their improvised invasion of Dalaran, the League of Explorers caught up with them in the tombs beneath Uldum, and it all climaxed with a pitched aerial battle in the skies above Northrend.

A narrative of that size required far more storytelling support than the average year. Previous years had normally seen three *Hearthstone* cinematics released; in 2019, Blizzard released twelve. There were the usual announcement cinematics, but each expansion also had short teaser cinematics, followed by another cinematic to set up the premise of the single-player adventure, where the real narrative twists and turns could be explored.

"We had to decide fairly quickly which format we wanted for those adventures," Nguyen said. "The Dungeon Run style had worked well for us the year before, but we also thought the old style of adventures would be great, too."

Kobolds & Catacombs had introduced the roguelike Dungeon Run adventure in 2017, and it had been an immediate hit. No *Hearthstone* adventure had ever felt so replayable before. Two expansions in 2018 had refined the format, and the new variety of bosses, heroes, and card mechanics kept players demanding more.

"We just weren't done with Dungeon Run yet," Nguyen said. "There were so many cool ideas that we had never gotten a chance to use, we decided to go all-in on them for the first two expansions."

PREVIOUS PAGES
Rafael Zanchetin

THIS PAGE
Dan Scott

THE DALARAN HEIST

THIS PAGE
Ludo Lullabi
& Sam Nielson

The first adventure of the year, *The Dalaran Heist*, showed how the League of E.V.I.L. conquered the city of Dalaran. Each of the five villains was responsible for subduing different districts. Obviously, the villains were too important to lead the assaults themselves, so they delegated the tasks to their underlings. Nine of the League of E.V.I.L.'s most ~~expendable~~ capable lieutenants answered the call, pitting their unique powers against a series of increasingly dangerous bosses. The more districts the player cleared, the more characters and Hero Powers they could choose from.

The Dalaran Heist also introduced a new twist: the Friendly Encounter. Every few rounds, players would take a quick break in one of Dalaran's many taverns, giving them a chance to modify their deck, buff their minions, or even cut loose cards they didn't want. No matter which tavern players entered, they were greeted by Bartender Bob, a friendly new face who offered cold drinks and conversation without judgment . . . even though, you know, you were playing as a criminal trying to invade his city.

"When we started hearing the voice lines for Bob," said Nguyen, "it was instantly perfect. I wasn't sure how his encouraging voice would actually feel in the middle of a Dungeon Run, but now we had this friendly father figure chatting with you. It was different. It was great."

To fill in the weeks between the single-player adventure and the next expansion, the designers began to experiment with limited-time Tavern Brawls that could continue the narrative.

Once the League of E.V.I.L. seized Dalaran, they had to fly all the way to Uldum. That's a long, long distance. It was very easy to imagine something going wrong. "Sure," said Chu, "the League of E.V.I.L. was effective enough to capture Dalaran, but that didn't mean they would be good at steering it."

After brainstorming several ideas about the problems a flying city could encounter, the designers created a limited-time Tavern Brawl called *Blackrock Crash*. Dr. Boom had sent Dalaran off course, crashing into Blackrock Mountain.

To wrestle the city free and get back on their way, the League of E.V.I.L. had to tangle with the armies of Ragnaros and Nefarian, who had starred in the 2015 adventure *Blackrock Mountain*.

Getting the Dungeon Run format up and running for a limited-time event was a herculean effort.

"For full adventures, you normally have a much longer scheduling pipeline," said Chu. "We weren't sure if we had the time to pull off *Blackrock Crash*, but the engineers managed to get it done."

TOMBS OF TERROR

For *Tombs of Terror*, the adventure accompanying the expansion *Saviors of Uldum*, the design team once again built a Dungeon Run, although with a much different approach. Instead of playing as one of nine evil lieutenants, players stormed the tombs of Uldum as the four starring members of the League of Explorers.

Unlike the League of E.V.I.L., the heroes had no qualms about getting their hands dirty.

And for the first time, a Dungeon Run would have progression mechanics. As players defeated more and more bosses, they'd unlock powerful treasures, Hero Powers, and junior Explorers to aid them. And once the junior Explorers got some experience under their belts, they'd get promoted to senior Explorers, with all the perks and benefits (and powers) that come with it.

"This was something we had wanted to try in Dungeon Runs for a long time," said Nguyen. "The roguelike genre is kind of hard-core. You fail? Game over. You're done. But the side effect is that if you get a bad start, you don't have much incentive to continue your run, since you probably won't win. Offering rewards for *any* progress meant you wanted to play things out."

Some of the unlockable rewards were quite powerful indeed, giving players who were stuck on a particular tomb a chance to overpower them if they kept trying. And multiple tries were almost certainly necessary; the final boss of each chapter was one of the Plague Lords—five terrifying monsters wielding world-ending power.

The fifth and final boss was a doozy of a fight. The four heroes of the League of Explorers had to bring all of their treasures and allies together against **Tekahn, Plague Lord of Flame**. With a health pool of 300 hit points and a deck of devastatingly unfair cards, he was almost impossible to beat in one go.

Fortunately, his health pool was persistent. The League of Explorers didn't have to kill him in one shot. They could wear him down, retreat, and return after upgrading more of their signature treasures. The persistent health pool mechanic had been used a couple of times, particularly in unique events for Fireside Gatherings, but never in a single-player mode.

And there was a friendly face amid all the fighting. The Friendly Encounter mechanic was too good to give up, and Bartender Bob was too charming to leave in Dalaran, so he traveled to Uldum before the League of Explorers. By the time they arrived, his taverns were already doing brisk business. Not even the Plague Lords seemed interested in interfering.

It wouldn't be the last time players saw Bartender Bob, of course.

Once the League of Explorers triumphed over the Plague Lords, they had to rush to Northrend. But, just as the League of E.V.I.L. had demonstrated, traveling via unfamiliar methods can cause all sorts of problems.

And the source of those problems was the faux mage, Reno Jackson.

"Yeah, he's not that good of a mage yet, but he does have a bunch of magic wands," said Chu. "What if he kept trying to open a portal to Northrend, but instead kept sending the Explorers to the wrong place?"

The Tavern Brawl event *Road to Northrend* was another take on the mini–Dungeon Run, drawing upon many bosses and locations from *Hearthstone*'s past. Every time the Explorers would defeat a boss, Reno would try to open another portal.

After defeating eight bosses, Reno would *finally* get them out of danger, but not without suffering a thousand insults from his colleagues.

LEFT & CENTER
Ludo Lullabi
and Sam Nielson

TOP RIGHT
Dark Pharaoh Tekahn
Ludo Lullabi
& Sam Nielson

OPPOSITE
Ludo Lullabi
& Sam Nielson

GALAKROND'S AWAKENING

Once the League of Explorers arrived in Northrend, they learned the League of E.V.I.L.'s true objective. As the teaser cinematic for *Descent of Dragons* showed, the villains wanted to raise something that had lain dormant in the snowdrifts of Dragonblight: the bones of Galakrond, the apocalyptic proto-dragon.

But more importantly, the finale of the yearlong narrative would try something new for the *Hearthstone* team—but something quite old for Blizzard itself.

The original *Warcraft: Orcs & Humans* had two campaigns. Choose to play the human side, and you'd destroy the orcs' war machine forever. Choose the orc faction, and you'd ransack Stormwind and drive the humans from their homes. Each ending meant different things for the world and the future of its characters.

So it would be in the *Descent of Dragons* single-player adventure, *Galakrond's Awakening*. Players could choose to lead the fearless heroes of the League of Explorers to victory and save the world . . . or side with the League of E.V.I.L. to unleash the might of Galakrond and help destroy Azeroth.

Galakrond's Awakening was also the first collection-based adventure since 2017's *Knights of the Frozen Throne*, where players used their own cards to build decks against challenging, predetermined boss fights.

"It's really hard to tell a proper finale through a Dungeon Run," said Nguyen. "Since bosses are randomized, you have limits on what you can do. We wanted to see specific characters facing off for the end of the Year of the Dragon."

The two different endings meant wildly different consequences for the characters and the world, which was part of the fun. Did you choose to ride Galakrond into battle and destroy the entire world? Or did you risk everything in a pitched battle against the biggest dragon the world has ever seen?

The choice was up to you.

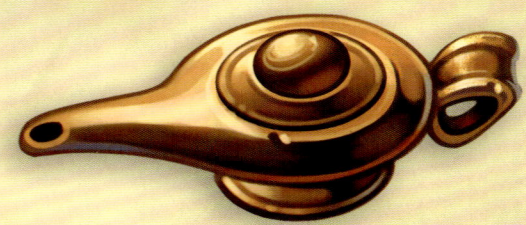

YOUR WISH IS MY SUGGESTION

Ask the *Hearthstone* team which card was the most difficult to make, and there's no debate: **Deathstalker Rexxar**, the hunter death knight hero from 2017's *Knights of the Frozen Throne*. By all accounts, it was the most complicated card that designers and engineers had ever attempted to implement.

Deathstalker Rexxar's Hero Power was Build-A-Beast: players would discover two beasts, and they would be combined into a single creature with cumulative health, attack, and card effects. It would have been hard enough to implement just using the cards in that expansion, but the team decided to keep updating Rexxar's Hero Power to account for new beasts in future sets, even long after he rotated out of Standard Format.

"That card gave us a lot of 'forever work,'" said senior designer Chadd Nervig. "As long as we release new cards, we'll be updating Rexxar's buckets of beasts. We really weren't excited about any new ideas that would put us in that position again."

Nevertheless, one of the cards in the *Saviors of Uldum* expansion not only threatened to match the complexity of Deathstalker Rexxar but to surpass it. In some ways, it did.

Zephrys the Great was a djinn with a unique Battlecry: *If your deck has no duplicates, wish for the perfect card.*

When completed, it required the most development time of any card in the game's history.

"Yeah, this one was crazy, but we were actually able to keep it in the realm of sanity," said Nervig.

The idea for the card started out even more bombastic, according to principal designer Peter Whalen. The original inspiration called for a genie-type character who would have allowed players to get any card they wanted.

"What if he could just open up your card collection and let you choose? How would that work?" said Whalen. "Well, we tried to figure it out."

The user interface team had some ideas on how to organize the card collection in the middle of a match, but the difference between playing on a desktop and a mobile phone made it a much bigger challenge.

"And then someone said, 'What if he just knows what the best card is and gives you that one?'" said Whalen.

That seemed a lot more manageable from a UI perspective, but it was daunting from a design and engineering standpoint. Perhaps it was even impossible, especially if every card that had ever been released—or that ever would be released—needed to be accounted for.

A limitation was quickly put into place: Zephrys could only consider cards from the Basic and Classic sets. There were so many effects across the nine different classes that players could find a solution to almost any scenario. Need to clear the board? Zephrys could show you **Twisting Nether** or **Flamestrike**, depending on the situation. Did your opponent just play a big beast of a minion that will kill you next turn? **Polymorph**.

But there were so many more scenarios. So many more possible board states. And a few edge cases that needed to be avoided.

"He never gives you anything like **Shadowstep** or **Youthful Brewmaster**, because you can't wish for more wishes," said senior designer Liv Breeden.

Designers and engineers had to tackle the problem head-on, filling up countless whiteboards with notes and design algorithms. The card not only had to judge the current board state; it had to consider the next turn as well, because the perfect card might require waiting for more mana before playing it.

"I think it took a couple of weeks to get a simple, clumsy version running as a prototype, but it took much, much longer to get it ready for release," said Breeden.

Even when the card was launched, it still required tuning, because players kept encountering unusual situations where Zephrys hadn't quite offered the perfect card. Even the patch notes describing the tweaks ran thousands of words.

"Even after all that work, it might be my favorite card of all time," said Whalen.

THESE PAGES
Max Grecke

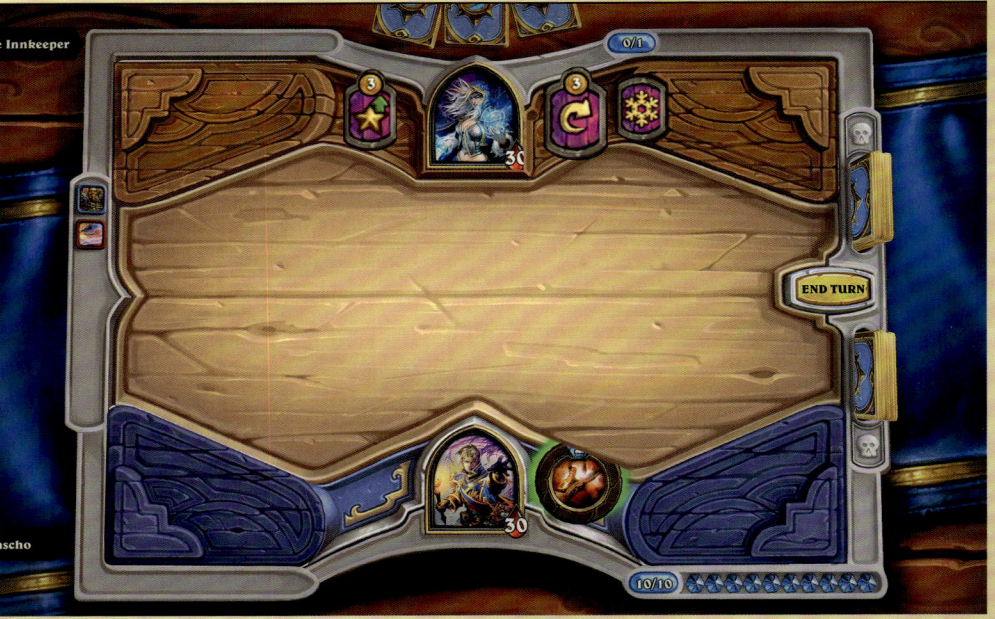

A NEW WAY TO PLAY

In early 2019, a new take on strategy games skyrocketed in popularity. Known as "auto battlers," players would place minions on a 3D grid and then unleash them in one-versus-one fights. The twist? The player would not directly participate; the minions would battle on their own based on positioning.

Hearthstone designers thought there could be a fun 2D twist on the concept, and so after *Rise of Shadows* launched, they began to play around with prototypes to see how it felt. The assumption was that it could make for a fun Tavern Brawl.

Once a playable prototype became available to the Hearthstone team, it was clear that this design was special.

"People started staying late at work to play it," said principal designer Peter Whalen. "Once the team realized how much fun this could be, everyone rallied behind it. Actually, come to think of it, this whole process was crazy. It came together so fast."

It wasn't until June 2019 that work on Battlegrounds was fully underway. Eight players would face off in a tournament-style competition, recruiting minions and constructing strategies that they hoped would leave them the sole victor among the lobby.

The existing production plan hadn't accounted for an entirely new game mode, and there were limitations on how much art and engineering time the team could spare to pursue their inspiration. Plus, the team had already begun work on sets for 2020, and it seemed risky to jeopardize those for this new game mode.

"We had to move smart and fast on this one," said lead UI/UX designer Max Ma. "It was one of the shortest development cycles I've ever been a part of."

The engineering team had a major challenge ahead of them. *Hearthstone* was built for one-versus-one fights, not eight-player lobbies. Scaling up was no easy feat, especially considering that all eight players would be recruiting minions from the same pool.

Almost all of the cards for the initial release of Battlegrounds came from existing sets, so the illustrations were already available. But the user interface for Battlegrounds had to diverge wildly from a Standard ranked match, while still looking like it belonged in *Hearthstone*.

Additionally, the minion card frames themselves needed to express different information than normal *Hearthstone* cards. Besides Health and Attack, cards also needed to show their Tavern Tier. The higher the tier, the more powerful the card, and the more damage it would do to its opponent if it survived a combat round.

The custom board for Battlegrounds had some surprising innovations. From the beginning, designers wanted a clear distinction between the Recruit phase and the Combat phase of gameplay. "For one mode, you have total control. For the other, you have no control at all," said Ma.

The Recruit phase was handled by Bartender Bob, the friendly presence in two adventures during the Year of the Dragon. Players would "shop his wares" and select useful minions for their next round of combat, or they could spend larger amounts of gold to upgrade their Tavern Tier in hopes of seeing even better choices.

"One of the early ideas was to have the Recruit board rolling out like a bazaar shopping stall, and Bob just lays everything out for you," said Ma.

But after an engineer experimented with another visual cue, the team shifted directions. "The combat board had a lot going on, and he made all of the corners flip upside down. It made the board clean," added Ma, "and it kept you focused on the Recruit phase. It was pretty well perfect."

By the middle of the summer, the team had a prototype that was shaping up into something polished and fun. Designers invited community content creators and streamers to get a sneak peek at the new mode and offer feedback on the way it played. Their suggestions were iterated upon quickly.

In just a few months, Battlegrounds would be playable on the floor of BlizzCon 2019, and by the middle of November, the game would be released in early access. It quickly became one of the most significant features ever made for *Hearthstone*, gaining a large and loyal audience.

The Battlegrounds development process had shown how much fun new game modes could be. Reinterpreting *Hearthstone*'s pillars had created a new way to play. And this would not be a one-off initiative.

By the time the Year of the Dragon ended, the team's designers were already hard at work playtesting even more wild new game modes. . . .

ABOVE
Charlène Le Scanff

OPPOSITE
Jerry Mascho

ABOVE
Waxrider Togwaggle
Konstantin Turovec

ABOVE
Cobalt Scalebane
Jim Nelson

ABOVE
Glyph Guardian
Konstantin Turovec

ABOVE
Steward of Time
James Ryman

ABOVE
Twilight Emissary
Mike Sass

ABOVE
Kalecgos, Arcane Aspect
Alex Horley

ABOVE
Dragonspawn Lieutenant
Luca Zontini

ABOVE
Kalecgos, Arcane Aspect
Alex Horley

ABOVE
Herald of Flame
Mauricio Herrera

ABOVE
Bronze Warden
Alex Garner

ABOVE
Drakonid Enforcer
Oliver Chipping

ABOVE
Unstable Ghoul
Mike Nicholson

OPPOSITE
Hangry Dragon
Hyo-Guen Ji

CONCLUSION

C'mon. Who did you choose? Did you help the good guys win, or did you let the villains run amok? Or did you try both, just to have some fun? You can tell me.

Ah. Fine. Keep your secrets.
It's all in good fun, anyways.

But since you're back, I have another riddle for you: "I fly on two wings, my claws are sharp. I'm bright as the sun, from ashes I'm wrought. I've lived and died, but still thrums my beating heart. What am I?"

That one's a little harder, eh? That's all right. Maybe I'm just not that talented at writing riddles.

But hey, before you go,
I've got some fun ideas for your next visit.

We can travel to a concert on a distant world.
We can head back to school to learn some spells.
Maybe we can even take a trip to the fair!

See you soon, friend!

Oh. The riddle. Right.
The answer to all those clues is . . .

. . . a phoenix.

—Harth Stonebrew, the Innkeeper

OPPOSITE, MIDDLE LEFT
Serpentine
Jason Kim

OPPOSITE, BOTTOM LEFT
Playing Koi
Will Murai

OPPOSITE, TOP RIGHT
Shoring Up
Charlène Le Scanff

OPPOSITE, MIDDLE RIGHT
Dame Hazelbark
Jomaro Kindred

OPPOSITE, BOTTOM RIGHT
Kul Tiras
Christopher Hayes

ABOVE
Blushroom
Charlène Le Scanff

ABOVE
Desert Bloom
Charlène Le Scanff

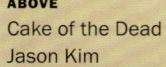

ABOVE
Cake of the Dead
Jason Kim

TOP LEFT
Banshee Queen
Katherine Fortune

MIDDLE LEFT
Pristine Scenes
Will Murai

BOTTOM LEFT
Got Away with It!
Jerry Mascho

TOP RIGHT
Legion Schemes
Chris Hayes

MIDDLE RIGHT
Machine Dreams
Chris Hayes

BOTTOM RIGHT
Awesome Blossom
Will Murai

TOP LEFT
Blizzard Events 2019
Katherine Fortune

MIDDLE LEFT
Sea of Dunes
Charlène Le Scanff

BOTTOM LEFT
League of Explorers
Charlène Le Scanff

TOP RIGHT
Darkmoon Faire
Katherine Fortune

MIDDLE RIGHT
The Shattering
Josh Harris

BOTTOM RIGHT
Titanic Tasks
Katherine Fortune

ABOVE
Card of Shadows
Charlène Le Scanff

249

TOP LEFT
Suramar
Charlène Le Scanff

MIDDLE LEFT
Stolen Thunder
Jerry Mascho

BOTTOM LEFT
Shado-Pan
Charlène Le Scanff

TOP RIGHT
Prize of Shadows
Jerry Mascho

MIDDLE RIGHT
Elise's Journal
Josh Harris

BOTTOM RIGHT
Jewel of Lazul
Josh Harris

ABOVE
Tomb Invader
Charlène Le Scanff

TOP LEFT
Book of Explorers
Charlène Le Scanff

BOTTOM LEFT
Book of E.V.I.L.
Charlène Le Scanff

TOP RIGHT
Dame Hazelbark
Jomaro Kindred

BOTTOM RIGHT
Hellfire Peninsula
Josh Harris

ABOVE
Year of the Dragon
Charlène Le Scanff

FOLLOWING PAGE
Twisted Knowledge
Rafael Zanchetin